How to Sell 100 Homes a Year

A Tactical Playbook

TIM STOUT

DEDICATION

To the love of my life, Christy. Thank you for always believing in me and my crazy dreams.

ACKNOWLEDGMENTS

Thanks to my dad, Bob, for being my prime supporter and mentor.

To my mother, Carla, thanks for having faith in me when no one else did, teaching me the love of reading and learning, and showing me what true love and compassion really are.

Thanks to my childhood best friend, Cliff, for always pointing me in the right direction.

To my first boxing coach, the late Marvin Fritts, thanks for teaching me the art of boxing and making me the fighter I am today.

To the late Cobb Riddle, a man of many talents, thanks for always seeking to bring out the best in me, inside and outside of the ring.

Thanks to Scott Martino, for saying "you should write a book" and believing in me even when I didn't.

Thanks to Ariel McCrory for bringing my lessons alive with this book, I couldn't have done this without your help and persistence.

Thanks to my real estate team for forcing me to level up every day, I'm so proud to be in business with you.

Thanks to my mentor and business coach, David Keesee, for challenging me and helping my dreams come true.

Finally, I'd like to thank everyone who lives in Mountain City, TN for helping me and believing in this small-town boy.

TABLE OF CONTENTS

FORWARD

In 2015, I met a man who had just gotten into the real estate business. He was a hustler. He had drive. He was hungry. He started with almost nothing and was spending some of his only dollars to invest in himself and his skills through our coaching.

Today that man sells hundreds of homes a year and is a linchpin in this Real Estate industry. It's a privilege to introduce you to a force in the realm of real estate, a dear friend, and a remarkable professional, Tim Stout.

Over the past decade, our paths have intersected in the dynamic world of real estate, where success stories are written with determination, expertise, and unwavering commitment.

In my tenure as a coach and mentor to over 40,000 real estate agents, I've encountered the spectrum of talent and ambition. Amid this landscape, Tim Stout stands tall as the epitcme of excellence—a member of the 1% of the 1%. I've had the honor of witnessing Tim's evolution, a journey marked by sheer dedication and an unyielding pursuit of mastery. From a humble beginning of 9 deals annually to orchestrating hundreds of transactions each year, Tim has not only rewritten the script but he's set a new standard in the industry.

His proficiency extends far beyond the conventional boundaries of real estate. Tim has unraveled the intricate threads of the game, embracing diverse facets—from facilitating seamless transactions for clients to astute investment strategies, to nurturing and guiding his team members into becoming top-tier producers in their own right.

What makes Tim's story both inspiring and instructive is not solely the magnitude of his accomplishments but the ethos that underscores his approach—integrity, genuine care for his clients, and a resolute pledge to excellence. His journey isn't merely about numbers but about the lives he's touched, the communities he's enriched, and the legacy he's building.

In this book, Tim generously shares the blueprint of his success, offering a roadmap crafted from years of invaluable experience, hard-earned wisdom, and a relentless pursuit of excellence. Through these pages, you'll not only gain insights into the mechanics of succeeding in real estate but also a glimpse into the mindset that propels one to the summit of achievement in this industry.

Prepare to embark on a transformative journey guided by a maestro in the realm of real estate. Tim Stout's books aren't just a guide; they are an invitation to elevate your practice, redefine your limits, and chart a course toward unparalleled success.

Tim, thank you for your trust in me, your friendship, your dedication, and your steadfast commitment to raising the bar. Your book is a testament to your passion for empowering others to achieve greatness. I'm so proud of you all you have become and it's crazy to think...the best is still yet to come.

Your coach, David Keesee

INTRODUCTION

Are you a real estate agent looking to take your business to the next level? This tactical playbook offers valuable insights and strategies that will help you achieve your goals, become a top-producing real estate agent, and develop your leadership skills. You will glean top-notch advice from this playbook on how to lead and motivate others; skills that will benefit both your career and personal growth. You will learn that standing out in the real estate industry means providing exceptional service to your clients so that you can create a positive reputation and generate repeat business and referrals. You will be able to recalibrate your mindset, streamline your processes and enhance your lead generation and closed deals. You will be able to create a positive culture and foster a strong work environment to increase your productivity and ultimately sell more homes….so let's begin!

The funnel diagram on the next page provides a visual aid for the flow of typical real estate business. Think of this funnel as a purifier. You can take any new business or non-functioning business, even a toxic business - and pour it through this purifying funnel to change the chemical makeup of the business and produce outstanding results.

Inside this diagram you'll find actionable techniques and skills to propel your real estate career to new heights. Each section of this tactical playbook carefully outlines this diagram to provide you with the influential knowledge needed to become a top-producing agent.

Mindset of Top Producer + System and Procedures

- Edu-Tainment
- Scripts & Objection Handling
- Working & Growing Your Sphere
- The Importance of Building Your List by Cold-Calling and CircleProspecting
- Velcro Prospecting to Sustain and Maintain

- Commit, Engage and Re-Engage
- Staying Top-of-Mind
- Retargeting Through Social Media
- Increasing the Quality, Increasing the Competition
- Setting Expectations

- How to Negotiate Without Being Offensive
- White Glove Service Through Turbulence
- Building Rapport & Maintaining Trust
- Treating the Co-op Agent as a Collaborator, Not a Competitor
- Transaction Coordination & Closings

Client Retention and Referrals

The wide rim of the funnel represents that all items of business must begin by flowing through a positive mindset and efficient systems and procedures. Without these at the beginning, nothing else will flow properly, and your results will not be pure, valuable, or long-standing. These set the stage for all the other action items to follow. The first two sections of the book will focus on building your tactical playbook with the mindset of a top-producer and the right systems and procedures, so that you will be ready to

—

transform your real estate business into a top-producing one by following the next stages of action steps.

The next stage of the funnel represents your clientele's journey through your resources, scripts, advertising, and prospecting to make sure that you are exhibiting top-notch lead follow-up and marketing for the business. Every item coming into your real estate business must be filtered through your communication, which builds your reputation. You can communicate through your lead nurturing - as well as your marketing and advertising to provide value to others and build your brand.

Once you have transformed your clientele to "stick" to you, the next stage of the funnel teaches you how to negotiate on their behalf, increase the quality of your service, and re-engage your clients and sphere to remain top-of-mind. As incoming business flows down the funnel, it must be filtered through the best quality and highest level of service to transform its chemical makeup into long-lasting client retention and name you as the local expert.

The final stage of the funnel teaches you how to build rapport with your clientele, maintain their trust as you collaborate with business affiliates to bring your transactions from contracts to closings. This is the final stage of the funnel for the purified experience.

After business has left your funnel, it can remain as long-lasting client retention and gain more referrals to start the filtration process again. However, if the final product isn't cared for correctly, it won't be retained. The last section of the book will review how to retain past clients and utilize them to gain more business through the funnel.

Throughout the book, there will be references to supplemental material provided for free, along with a community of other entrepreneurs for you to join. You will be invited to visit our Facebook Group community to join the movement and access more resources, and I hope you take advantage of these opportunities. I also invite you to read my other book when you're done with this one, *Forged in Fire: 50 Fighting Tactics to Help Your Business Succeed,* which offers business practices and mindsets to train leaders to unleash their potential and achieve their goals, so that you can take ownership of your life and business.

To join the Facebook Community of other readers and entrepreneurs who are also utilizing these tactics and the extra resources provided within the group, you can scan this QR code.

 To read the e-Book, Audio book, or Hardcopy of *Forged in Fire: 50 Fighting Tactics to Help Your Business Succeed*, you can scan this QR code.

The following chapters will guide you through the process of building your tactical playbook and implementing the right action plans so that you'll be prepared to take your real estate business to the next level and become a top-producing agent. Get ready to elevate your success and achieve your goals!

PART 1 - MINDSET OF A TOP PRODUCER

Feeling tired and stressed every day? Overwhelmed by negativity and negative self-talk? It might be because your attention is focused on things that don't really matter for you or your business. These distractions can take away precious time and energy from activities that actually generate income. In order to succeed, you'll need to prioritize income-producing tasks, invest in training, contribute to your community, and align with the mission and vision of your business. Top-producers stop wasting time and energy on things that don't matter and focus on what matters most for their business. To do this, you must believe in yourself and your abilities. Remember, what you focus on becomes magnified in your life.

In order to strengthen your business and boost your willpower muscle, you must first learn to focus only on what truly matters. In my book, *Forged in Fire: 50 Fighting Tactics to Help Your Business Succeed*, I introduce the concept of "minding what matters." We're all familiar with the saying "mind over matter," but what about "mind what matters?" This powerful mindset shift can help you ignore distractions and employ laser-focus on what truly counts for success.

Mind what matters and do not mind what does not matter. Don't let negativity and self-doubt hold you back. Instead, focus on positive truths by shifting your mindset away from the negativity and towards your goals, the future, and positive thinking. When you shift your mindset, you'll see incredible results in your life.

By strengthening your willpower, you'll experience a remarkable increase in its potency and discover the unbelievable impact of focusing on what truly matters. Embracing positivity will also infuse your life with a newfound sense of optimism.

On the flip side, indulging in negativity can lead to a downward spiral, alienating others and even yourself. What you choose to focus on will inevitably be amplified in your life. Therefore, it's vital to mindfully select your focus.

In this section, you'll learn how to cease wasting valuable time and instead prioritize actions that yield the desired results. Rather than wasting time and energy, you'll start investing it! With a greater understanding of what truly matters for you and your business, success will follow suit. Choose wisely what you focus on, for it shall shape your reality.

Chapter 1 - The Friction Theory

No one else chooses happiness or sadness for us - we each choose them on our own. Happiness can naturally lead to more positivity, and sadness increases negativity. Positivity is like a muscle that must be exercised, and cannot be trusted on its own. We have to decide what we will feel, and the more positive we choose to feel then the more enhanced our lives will become. The stronger the muscle gets, the easier it is to make the decision to remain in a positive mindset.

Practicing extreme ownership over your situation can be so difficult at times, especially when we get stuck in the quicksand of our comfort zone or negativity. Sometimes we make it harder on ourselves than it really needs to be and we fail to execute our positivity muscle into action. We can get so overwhelmed by the beast of change that it keeps us from taking the first step. What if it were easier to make bigger changes in our lives? When we break down our goals into small changes and start implementing them into our routine, we can adjust the trajectory of our future in very big ways. Just like when a pilot flies a plane, the slightest change in direction can make a major difference in the long-term journey. If the nose of the airplane is adjusted by a few feet, the passengers may not notice at first. But this will end up changing the plane's destination by miles and miles.

Staying in the same rut of routines can be harmful and lead us to become stagnant, both in our business and personal lives. With courage and a bit of effort, making large changes to our routines and mindset can be just what we need to break through to the next level. Even helping us reconnect with what truly matters most in our lives, whether that means spending more time with family or having the energy to do something else we're passionate about. The possibilities are vast when we take that initial step towards transformation and implement the small routines and habits that will lead to greater action.

Implementing new habits is rudimentary to our growth and we do it by focusing on small changes and their long-term effects. This helps us create positive outcomes that we may never have envisioned before. The key is to break down the goals into achievable tasks. For example, if you have a goal of running regularly, the best thing you can do for yourself when you get ready in the morning is to put your running clothes on. Then it will be more likely that you will follow through with the goal instead of allowing yourself to push it off indefinitely. It might seem like a small step, but taking this small action every day will make it easier to keep up with your goal and have a sense of accomplishment at the end of each day when the goal has been met.

When it comes to making big changes in our lives and reaching our goals, sometimes adding friction can be the most transforming component of creating success. The notion of adding friction has been cited by many experts, from business professionals to authors. When we add just a little bit more friction consistently, we have the potential to create lasting results and reach our goals one step at a time. Just like we can make it easier for ourselves to meet our goals by adding certain friction, we can also make it harder on ourselves when friction arises that we were not prepared to face. That is why it is revolutionizing to regularly train ourselves into choosing a positive mindset with discipline, so that we can wisely handle objections that may otherwise inhibit us from reaching our goals. Don't buy ice cream or have desserts in your house if your goal is to lose weight. Don't sleep with your phone next to your bed if your goal is to lessen your screen time. Adding friction against what you want is an excellent way to build the will-power muscle.

Motivation comes and goes, but strengthening the will-power muscle can be done with consistent decisions, habits, and routines to make small changes and create big results. If you are willing enough not to smoke for three days, then you know you can make it three days without smoking. Now there's a measurable length to create and conquer another goal, so that you can willpower through a longer time period. Keep adjusting the trajectory by making smaller tasks for yourself to keep your goals.

Friction creates pressure. Negative pressure that comes from comparing ourselves to others, or from a toxic mindset can lead us to ruin dreams and relationships. But positive pressure can push us out of our comfort zone. So ready, aim, and fire - readjust any negative pressure to positive pressure by focusing on growth, strength, and getting to a better place so that you can help others get there as well.

Mental strength needs to be continually strengthened. Sometimes extreme heat or extreme cold can help strengthen mental strength, specifically by doing something you do not want to do in order to gain mastery over it. Add friction and positive pressure first to your personal life, and you'll be on your way to building this in your business life as well.

Have you ever found yourself making excuses for why you haven't achieved your goals? Maybe you've blamed external factors, like a lack of resources or bad timing. But the truth is, the real reason you're not succeeding is because you're not taking extreme ownership. We're all guilty of this at various stages in our personal growth. Extreme ownership means taking full responsibility for your actions, decisions, and outcomes. It means acknowledging that no matter what happens, you have the power to control your own success. When you take extreme ownership, you stop making excuses and start taking action.

Making excuses is easy. It's a simple way to avoid accountability and deflect blame. But it's also a major roadblock to success. If you're constantly making excuses, you're not looking for solutions. You're not taking action. You're just making it easier for yourself to quit. So, what are some common excuses that people make? Here are a few that I hear often:

- Lack of resources: "I don't have enough money/time/resources to make it happen."

- Bad timing: "It's just not the right time for me to start this project."
- No support: "I don't have anyone who believes in me or my ideas."
- Lack of skill: "I'm just not good enough to make it happen."

These excuses are limiting beliefs. They are holding you back from achieving your goals. The truth is, you can overcome these obstacles with the right mindset and determination. You can find ways to make it happen, no matter what. So, how can you take extreme ownership and stop making excuses? Don't rely on others to solve your problems. Remember, we each choose for ourselves how we feel and what we do every day. You can get creative and look for solutions instead of excuses. Brainstorm ways to overcome obstacles and find resources. This will cause you to take action with a positive mindset instead of waiting for the perfect opportunity in a complacent mindset. When we start working on goals now and adjust along the way, we can quickly launch our business forward. Stop blaming others and take responsibility for your own actions and decisions.

Surround yourself with supportive people and seek out more people who believe in you and your ideas. You truly become the medium of the five people you hang around the most, so instead of adopting a victim mentality or surrounding yourself with others who do not support your goals, surround yourself with unmatchable work ethic and wisdom. Hard workers and entrepreneurs. These are the folks who take extreme ownership.

The real estate world can be a difficult one at times and it requires skill, discipline and massive action to succeed. This builds the foundation to a top producer and it all begins with the decision to choose positivity and a disciplined mindset. Believing that you are a top-producer before your bank account reflects it. Taking extreme ownership is the key to success and it means accepting responsibility for your outcomes and making a commitment to take action. So don't let excuses hold you back from achieving your goals. Start taking extreme ownership today and watch your success soar!

CHAPTER 2 - FAILING FORWARD

Once we have a positive mindset and disciplined actions stabilized, then we must remember that falling does not always mean failing. When we take our moments of "falling" and transform them into lessons that can launch our business forward, then we win. We don't fail. Learning to use our "failures" as victories in our business growth is the key to building an unshakeable business and real estate career.

How do we do this? Well, when we surround ourselves with coaches and mentors who can help direct us into a better trajectory, we ensure that the nose of our airplane continues facing up and forward in a better direction than we may know to steer it ourselves. Finding a business mentor, especially in real estate, can be a daunting task. But with the right research and guidance, you can find just the right mentor who can train you to streamline your business and expand your horizons. Let's dive into some quick tips on finding a business mentor who can help you "fail forward" so you don't have to reinvent the wheel as you're building your real estate business.

First you need to identify your goals. What is the purpose of having a mentor for you, to recruit more agents to your team or to streamline your systems and procedures? Are you looking for advice about starting a team or just growing your real estate production? Do you need help developing a strategy to reach new customers or expanding to a new market? Once you've identified what you want out of a mentor or real estate coach, then you can start looking for one who fits those criteria.

Before committing to anyone, you'll need to do some research on the batch of potential mentors you've found. What industry do they specialize in - leadership, sales, operations, or real estate? What experience do they have? Do they have an online presence where you can learn more about them and their expertise? This step will help you choose wisely. Once you have researched potential mentors, you'll want to reach out to your network of business contacts and ask around for potential mentors. Talk to people who are in the same or similar industries as yourself and find out who they might recommend. You may be surprised by what connections you make, and if the same name keeps coming up then it makes your decision easy!

There are also many online resources available to help you find the right mentor for your needs. For example, LinkedIn has a mentorship feature where you can connect with mentors in various industries. Using online platforms to vet potential mentors is a great way to narrow down your list of options.

When interviewing potential mentors, you'll want to make sure to ask the right questions. What successes have they had in their career? What challenges have they faced and how did they overcome them? Their successes and challenges may tell you more about how they think, and will help you decide if a mentor is the right fit for your needs.

At the end of the day, you don't have to commit to a real estate coach or mentor if they don't feel right for you. Take your time to make sure the coach is a good fit, and don't be afraid to say no. You can keep looking until you find someone who you feel confident can help you achieve your goals.

Even if a business coach or mentor has different ideas and approaches to business than you, it may be beneficial to learn from them and incorporate their strategies into your business. Keep an open mind as you're searching for the right one.

Before meeting with a potential mentor, you will want to take time to review your goals that you outlined, and see how the mentorship relationship can help you achieve these goals. Having a clear understanding of what you want out of the meeting can help ensure that both parties are getting the most out of the experience.

Then after meeting with a mentor, make sure to follow up with them and thank them for their help. Showing gratitude will go a long way in establishing a good relationship and can even lead to more opportunities down the line.

Once you've found the right business coach or mentor, commit yourself to keep learning. Make sure to continue developing your skills. Use the resources they provide to stay on top of industry trends and always strive for improvement. Listen to their direction and advice, it can only help you.

Finding a business mentor is a concrete way to gain insight into the business world and grow as an entrepreneur. So don't be afraid to reach out and ask questions. It will help you skip unnecessary mistakes and fail faster with the necessary mistakes to grow faster. This will push you to take more massive actions to become the local expert.

Remember, failure is a critical part of the learning process. It is often viewed as negative and something to be avoided, but it is a valuable experience that provides opportunities for growth and development. Instead of dwelling on a failure, you should use it as an opportunity to move forward and improve. Especially since failure is a natural part of life and something that every person will experience at some point. It can take many forms and while it is unpleasant and often uncomfortable, it is a chance to reflect on what went wrong and what can be done differently in the future. It will also allow you to gain new insights and perspectives, develop resilience and persistence, and strengthen your determination to succeed. It will help you build character and learn valuable life lessons that you can use in other areas of your life if you allow it to teach you.

Failing forward uses failure as a springboard for growth and improvement. It turns a negative experience into a positive one by learning from it and using that knowledge to make positive changes in the future. This requires a shift in perspective and a willingness to embrace failure as a natural part of the learning process to lead to more success.

Now if we're failing forward, where exactly is forward and by what measurements will we track our success? Success doesn't have to be financial and can mean something different for everyone. It is always fluid and moving. But if you focus on these questions, you can actively change the way you think and categorize your successes to help you measure where you're moving forward.

These questions create a strategy that can help you fail forward and turn a negative experience into a positive one when you can reflect on what went wrong, set new goals, and take action to improve. Seek support from friends, family, (and a mentor!), as they can provide valuable perspective and guidance.

- What went wrong?
- What were the solutions?
- How can this help me grow now & in the future?
- Do I need to adjust my goals because of a setback?
- Who are the people that I am surrounding myself with?
- What am I consuming in my work and free time?
- What type of conversations am I having?
- Are these people, tasks, and conversations pulling me closer to my goals and objectives, or farther from them?

When you ask these questions, you will have a clearer idea of where you are going and how you can use your "failing forward" to recalibrate yourself to your goals and destination.

The fear of failure is a common obstacle that prevents people from taking risks and trying new things. To overcome this fear, understand that failure is not a permanent condition and that everyone experiences it at some point. You can also use visualization and positive self-talk to help boost your confidence and overcome the fear of failure. It is a natural part of the learning process, and with the right perspective and strategies, you can turn it into a valuable tool for personal growth and success. If you fail - you learn. Sometimes a failure can be a better lesson than if it didn't happen to us, if it causes us to improve. Keep asking yourself these questions and they'll help keep you oriented around moving forward (and not backward) even through our "failures."

Chapter 3 - The Journey of 1,000 Miles

Stepping out of our comfort zone is a journey of personal growth and achievement. When we embrace the initial doubts and discomfort, they pale in comparison to the triumph we feel once we conquer the challenge.

We all know that saying - "the journey of 1,000 miles starts with 1 step." But have you ever stopped to think about what it really means?

It's simple. Every big, challenging journey we embark on in life - whether it's personal growth, career aspirations, or even improving our health and fitness - all begins with that fundamental first step. In this fast-paced world, it's easy to feel overwhelmed by the enormity of our goals. But by recognizing the power of taking that small, but significant, first step, we set ourselves up for success.

Start small and dream big. When we embrace the power of that first step, we ignite our personal growth, achieve career goals, and even revamp our own wellness and fitness routine.

When a mountain climber is scaling a mountain, they may not feel like they're making much progress at first. They may only be moving a few inches at a time, and the summit may seem like it's still far away. But every step taken is still forward progression. As long as they stay consistent and keep moving forward, no matter how small their steps may be. They will eventually reach the top of the mountain.

Don't let fear hold you back from truly living. Because in reality, fear doesn't prevent death, it prevents life. So when you're moving inches at a time, you're still making forward progress if you stay consistent.

Being scared to lose only wastes time. And regret is worse. Because results don't care about your motivation. Results concern your discipline. And discipline beats motivation every day. Choose discipline over motivation for your journey of 1,000 in your real estate career, you will need it.

When you're feeling discouraged or like you're not making much progress, remember that the journey of 1,000 miles is all about consistency and action. The key to success on any journey, no matter how long or difficult it may seem, is to start with a small step and stay consistent. Remind yourself of the vision and the steps that it will take to get you there. Soon the training and action steps will become easier and less of a challenge. Just keep moving forward, no matter how small your steps may be, and soon enough you will see the progress you've made and be proud of how far you've come.

I'll never forget the moment when my real estate team had 20 pending contracts on our hands. It was chaotic. Our systems were in shambles, unable to handle the load. Clearly, our procedures were not up to par for growth.

But we didn't settle for mediocrity. We decided to revamp our systems and push ourselves beyond our comfort zone. And it worked. By scaling our procedures and taking on the challenge, we were able to scale our business too. Sure, our old way of doing things was comfortable when we had fewer transactions. But we knew that comfort wouldn't cut it when we aimed for 50 transactions. Downsizing is easy, but expanding takes guts.

If you're serious about growth, you need to embrace the discomfort. Challenge yourself to scale your systems and procedures to meet your business's needs. This isn't something someone else can do for you. It's up to you to level up and cultivate the willpower to step outside your comfort zone.

Achieving greatness and high levels of success requires stepping out of your comfort zone and being challenged past your limiting beliefs. After your journey of 1,000 steps - though challenging and uncomfortable it may be at first, once you reach the place where you have taken action steps to carry out goals and implemented better systems and procedures, like wheels they will take you farther at a quicker pace. You'll see the success that comes with a scalable business. So don't settle for your current level of success, strive to climb a 10,000-step journey. Continuously challenge your thinking and the systems you implement to take your business to the next level. Don't get too comfortable, always push ahead, grow, and seek new ways to challenge your successful business. Your success and that of your team is deeply connected to your vision of growth, so let that vision be the driving force behind your collective achievements.

Taking that first step is necessary when pursuing personal goals and striving for success. Even if you fail, you'll learn and grow in ways you never thought possible. And don't worry about how fast you're going, as long as you keep moving forward consistently. This is the secret to building a scalable and successful business. Don't let your ambitions remain dreams. Take risks, push boundaries, and constantly seek new opportunities. You can experience growth and accomplishment by stepping outside your comfort zone. Overcome doubt and discomfort to taste the sweet success of a completed challenge. Remember, even the longest journeys begin with just one step.

CHAPTER 4 - CALIBRATING OUR SCHEDULE FOR SUCCESS

Just like we must resist the temptation to become too fixated on keeping up with a song's fast beat when we're working out - or else we'll train to someone else's rhythm and not our own - we must also find a pace and intensity level that works for us individually. In business, we have to learn to discipline ourselves according to our own goals and not someone else's to set a pace towards our own desired outcome. Focus on your own breathing to create a more sustainable tempo during your business development. This begins by calibrating your own schedule for success.

The three habits as a new real estate agent that you must embrace to be successful are:

- Waking up early to plan your day
- Writing down your goals (This helps them become real!)
- Time blocking your schedule

In our hectic and demanding lives, our time is a precious commodity. With countless responsibilities vying for our attention, it's easy to feel overwhelmed and lose sight of what truly matters. Juggling countless responsibilities and endless distractions can also leave us feeling scattered and unproductive. That's why having a foolproof time management system in place is absolutely key; it is a skill that we can no longer afford to overlook.

When we wake up early and plan our day ahead of time, we actually add hours into our day and start off the mornings being in control. If you control your mornings, you control your days. When you control your actions, you take control of your goals. Our goals can't just be a far-off hope- in order for them to be achievable, they have to be tangible. We must make them living and breathing and work them into our everyday life. We can do this by writing them down every morning - or reading them every morning.

What is time blocking? Time blocking is a technique where you dedicate a specific block of time to a specific task. By doing this, you ensure that you have enough time to complete the task without being distracted or derailed by other tasks. This method helps you stay focused on what you need to do and avoids wasting time on distractions. To start using time blocking, you need to make a schedule. You can start by creating a list of the tasks that you need to complete in a day. Next, prioritize these tasks and categorize them as A (must do), B (should do), or C (could do). Then allocate specific blocks of time to each task. For example, you could spend the first two hours of your day working on A tasks, followed by two hours for B tasks and the remaining time for C tasks.

Time blocking is a powerful tool, but it is not enough on its own to get us where we need to be. To maximize efficiency, you need to leverage the time you have available. This means finding ways to automate or delegate tasks that are taking up too much of your time. For example, if you find that you spend a lot of time on emails, you could use template emails to expedite this task, or use a tool like Boomerang to schedule your emails to be sent at a later time. This will free up your time for other tasks.

Time blocking and leveraging are powerful tools that can help you make the most of your time and get the results you want while making time for what matters in your schedule. This helps prioritize our "A"s, "B"s, and "C"s to complete them in order of importance for our income producing activities. (We'll talk more about this prioritization in chapter 7, on Lead Generation & Prospecting.) And if you expand to form a real estate team, managing and holding accountable those around you to leverage their tasks will help with the team's overall prioritization.

As a solo real estate agent, it is still important to manage and hold others accountable around you as well. This will help streamline your transactions for your clients and build lasting relationships with your business partners when you set an example for others to follow. This means having open and honest communication and setting clear expectations for what you need from those around you. Remind them of upcoming deadlines, stages in the transaction, and what will need to happen before the transaction closes. And if you need someone to help you with a task, set a deadline and make sure they understand the job scope and their responsibilities. This will ensure that everyone is on the same page and working towards the same goal.

But it all starts by taking control of your mornings and setting yourself up for a successful day, since your morning routine determines whether you'll have a productive day or a lazy one. By hitting the snooze button, you're giving yourself an excuse to procrastinate and lack discipline throughout the day. But if you wake up and start your day with purpose, you're laying the foundation for success.

If you're in a management position or an entrepreneurial role, treat each morning as if you're unemployed and seeking a new employer. Use that motivation to go out and find new business opportunities. Don't wait for business to come to you; be proactive and take control of your morning to generate leads and build your client base.

Create a strict morning routine that keeps you on track for a productive day. Whether it's hitting the gym, reading business books, or time-blocking your schedule, prioritize the tasks that will push your business forward. Complete the big and dreaded tasks first, just like Brian Tracy suggests in his book, "Eat the Frog." Your morning is your time to shine, so protect it like it's sacred. By owning your morning, you own the day, the weeks, months, and ultimately, your life.

Don't forget to prioritize your marketing efforts as well. When you spend the first few hours of your work morning on marketing, prospecting, and generating more business, then you are planning for tomorrow's business and ensuring long-term success. Prepare for the future and support tomorrow's business first.

Starting your morning off strong, refocusing on your goals and time-blocking and leveraging are powerful tools that can help you manage your time and make the most of your day. By prioritizing tasks, dedicating specific blocks of time to each task, leveraging your time, and managing and holding others accountable, you can achieve great results and make time for what truly matters.

Reclaim control over your life. Learn how to prioritize tasks, minimize distractions, and optimize your productivity. Don't let time slip through your fingers – take charge and make the most of every moment. Your success depends on it.

To access an example of a time-blocked schedule template, join our Facebook group community by scanning this QR code.

Chapter 5 - Taking Action

As a new real estate agent or a seasoned team leader, it is notable to remember that hard work is more important than talent in creating successful outcomes. Strong foundations are built when everyone focuses on their responsibilities and puts in the effort needed to achieve success. To ensure you and your team succeed, it's elemental to nurture your people first by creating an environment of trust and respect. Everyone needs to feel valued, inspired, and encouraged to perform at their best.

The following three traits make a good real estate agent into an excellent one, and sets the foundation for them to grow into a team leader:

- a sense of urgency,
- a willingness to help people,
- and a problem-solving mindset.

A great real estate agent needs to have the drive to stay ahead of competitors and understand how to advocate for their clients and team. They need to identify potential issues quickly and work with their business affiliates to find solutions that benefit everyone involved.

A hands-on agent should demonstrate empathy, provide support and guidance, and be willing to take risks. They need to have the ability to motivate those around them to reach their highest potential, while also exploring new strategies and solutions. As the agents grows into a team leader, they should make sure that team members feel empowered and valued while also providing constructive criticism and feedback.

The key is to become indispensable in the process so that you won't be replaced. While a mechanic can easily replace a broken wrench, it's much harder to replace a skilled mechanic.

When we focus on becoming a required piece of our industry, we secure our position for the long term. We do this by taking massive actions to develop our own problem-solving skills, communication, and leadership.

Simply opening doors and filling out paperwork will soon be a job for machines or exceptional agents who also provide value and skill. To truly make an impression on clients, staff members in real estate must play a critical role in the process. Team leaders also have the power to make a lasting impact on their teams, potentially changing lives and shaping futures.

Become an invaluable asset, not just a cog in the machine. Offer unique contributions that machines and others cannot. Share wisdom, experience, and expertise. Prioritize the client's needs and deliver exceptional customer service. Devote yourself to community and charity work, and build your business by tackling the tasks that others avoid or overlook.

As you take massive action in these areas, you'll begin to grow from your own solo-agent production to selling 100 homes a year and leading a team of others doing the same. A new agent should start taking actions to exemplify a team leader in their business now to naturally grow into that role and trajectory.

Make it crystal clear that your team is dedicated to the clients' best interests. Show everyone that your team members are not mere tools, but valuable contributors throughout the entire process. Empower your team to prioritize the clients' needs. This will guarantee that your team members are seen as needed components of the system, rather than just cogs in the machine.

Team leaders should be available and reachable for their team members. Making sure that questions are answered quickly and that team members have access to the resources they need can help to create an environment of trust and collaboration.

Leaders should also look for ways to show appreciation when a job is done well, as this helps to foster a sense of accomplishment and encourages team members to continue striving for excellence.

By recognizing the hard work their team puts in, team leaders can inspire their team to push themselves further and do even better in the future. At my company, I make sure my sales and administration staff know just how central they are to keeping things running smoothly. I constantly remind them that they are game changers for our business. Each person has a unique role to play, and without them, our business would crumble. They are the key to our team's triumph.

When team leaders build meaningful relationships with their team members, they can better understand each person's strengths and weaknesses, as well as their personal goals. This also means taking the time to actively listen to everyone's ideas and valuing them equally regardless of rank or seniority. Focus on enhancing the real estate culture around you by taking actions that reflect hard work, consistency and positivity. From there, you can then focus on the business and on giving it the attention and protection it needs so that everyone can benefit from its successes. When we put in the necessary groundwork, we can watch everything bloom.

Leaders need to maintain business-like communication and stay organized. This ensures that everyone is working towards clearly defined objectives and staying on track with their overall mission. It's also suitable for real estate agents and leaders to stay up-to-date with recent industry trends and events to inform decisions and provide invaluable advice for their clients and team members. With the right amount of dedication and guidance, they can make sure that everyone involved feels respected and motivated to do their best work.

The leaders and business owners who embody humility inspire others to grow and succeed more than the leaders who employ fear-based tactics to lead their teams. Throughout history, the greatest leaders have shown the way through their actions and words, stimulating others to follow suit. Pastors and parents alike have led by example, demonstrating the utmost humility and guiding their congregations and children towards greatness. This unique style of leadership demands a deep sense of humility and a willingness to lead through action. Whether it's tackling big or small tasks, these leaders step up and set the bar for others to aspire to. Gain the trust of your team by setting the right example in your words and actions.

The more fearful someone is on becoming a leveled-up leader or a local real estate expert, the more they prevent themselves from doing more in life. We can end the game of comparing ourselves to others (social media is the worst about this!) when we aim to take actions to be the best leaders and skilled experts that we can be... even if we don't have anyone around us to lead yet. These actions will keep aiming at our target to keep the plare soaring to its final destination.

By developing these traits, good real estate agents can become skilled and indispensable experts and distinct team leaders. They can inspire and motivate those around them to achieve excellence in all that they do. With an emphasis on communication, collaboration and problem-solving, these agents can create teams that are driven to succeed and equipped with the skills to make it happen. By demonstrating a sense of urgency, compassion and problem-solving abilities, they can ensure that their actions are well-equipped to take on the challenges ahead.

Part 2 - Systems & Procedures

Are you stuck in a repetitive cycle, completing tasks out of habit and without giving them a second thought? It's time to break free and discover the path to maximum efficiency. In our daily routines, we often complete tasks without much thought or consideration. It's only when someone points out a flaw or suggests a more efficient approach that we realize we can work smarter. Whether it's a small task or a long-standing habit, embracing structure and efficiency can save us time and energy in the long run. Accepting constructive criticism and implementing new strategies can transform us from good workers to exceptional leaders.

But how do we learn these ways of working? It begins with an openness to feedback and guidance from those who have mastered productivity. We must learn to listen carefully and implement constructive criticism from authorities and superiors. By doing so, we can cultivate our skills and become efficient workers, paving the way to becoming great leaders in the future. Don't settle for good when you can be great. You can start working smarter, not harder, today.

When we seize the opportunity to enhance our productivity and set ourselves up for success, we unlock efficiency. This teaches us to become good, efficient workers before we can become great leaders. Remember, when good meets great, good is simply not enough. The pursuit of greatness never ends – there is always someone better. Your mission must be to seek out those who are greater and challenge yourself to become even better. Don't be complacent, even if you dominate your market or have no competition. The competition will come, and if you're not prepared, they will surpass you. Get ready to compete or get left behind. Start fighting now for the win.

In my book, *Forged in Fire: 50 Fighting Tactics to Help Your Business Succeed*, I provide various applications on why it is best to have systems and procedures in place for everything to be done right the first time, or as close to it as possible the first time. Maximize productivity and avoid redundant work by ensuring your team doesn't duplicate tasks. This helps eliminate the need for redoing or reviewing paperwork and tasks and saves valuable time. Empower your team to work efficiently in their assigned tasks and systems, while being open to better systems suggested by others. This will streamline your workflow to avoid redundant tasks and rework, and will also foster a culture of continuous improvement.

You can learn to leverage systems and procedures to maximize your time and productivity by avoiding redundancy. Your time is invaluable and cannot be regained, so make every moment count. Treat your time like you treat your finances - invest it wisely. Just as you would aim to be efficient with your money, strive to work efficiently the first time around.

This section will briefly dissect some of your most profitable systems and procedures that will build the foundation for your top-producing real estate business. You'll be astounded by the enhanced productivity and success of your business when you prioritize efficiency, and both you and your team will witness a significant boost in overall productivity for your business.

CHAPTER 6: MARKETING

The two reasons that a home doesn't sell in a timely manner are because it is under-marketed or overpriced. When we make sure that the most eyes have seen the property, we guarantee that the price doesn't limit the buyers. Real estate agents must market, market, market. Excellent marketing is alone the best strategy to get the seller the most money and the best terms for the house. Pricing below market price drives buyer demand, while also driving up the price with multiple offers. Keep this in mind to price it strategically, then market strategically to obtain this result.

By far, the best improvement that anyone can do to maximize their current profit is to employ a top-notch marketing plan. The more serious the marketing, the better the pricing strategy will be for the home, and the stronger the pricing strategy is, then the more profit is maximized.

Capitalizing on marketing is the best way to raise buyer demand in the housing market. Taking the money that would normally be spent in 3-6 months on a marketing funnel and pouring it into a 30-day marketing blitz creates a massive action and immediately increases results. If you're not seeing the results you want, then your changes haven't been big enough. Rushing to properties builds up buyer demand and this is done through enhanced marketing. Marketing plans for your services and yourself are just as helpful as the ones you use for your listings. If folks don't know you're in the business, you won't remain top-of-mind.

Do not lose any time when it comes to marketing. Shoot it across all avenues. Use flyers in door knocking the neighborhood, mail out postcards to mailboxes, use radio, social media, newspaper and cold calls. Attract all the eyes to the property and to your services as an agent! This increases the foot traffic to the property and the omnipresence for your brand. You can measure your actions and marketing to see if you are receiving a positive or negative return on your investment, then you can make appropriate changes. Remember, nothing happens if nothing changes.

In terms of both your services and your client's listing, the best question to ask yourself in your marketing plan is: What problem are you solving for the consumer, and what value can you give them? Let's briefly talk about home advertising. If there is a high demand for swimming pools, then focus your advertising to buyers highlighting the pool feature of the home. Help the buyer fall in love with the house and outside curb appeal. Encourage the seller to paint their mailbox or install a new post if it looks older, or plant flowers around the mailbox.

Create a space that is inviting, comfortable and clean. The home and walkways should be pressure washed. The lawn should be manicured and freshly cut - with colorful flowers and pine if the season permits it. By the time the buyer even walks inside, they should already be in love with the outside of the home. Then on the interior, everything should be fresh-smelling, painted, and not cluttered. It should look welcoming, possibly renovated, neat, clean and in order. Get people through the door and they'll start making offers. Multiple offers. Don't price it too high that people would think something is wrong with the house if it sits for too long, but not too low where the seller would be leaving money on the table. This requires an understanding of the current market's trends and local demands.

Conduct a comparative market analysis for what the property should sell for, then maybe drop a smidge below that number to make it "a good deal" depending on the type of market you are in. People want to win and they get competitive, so this can help drive up multiple offers. Then you can drive the offers to above the appraised value, and push for the highest and best offer! But the house needs to be show ready, and priced appropriately for your market. You need to know what buyers are looking for and the best way to maximize profit for the seller. Then you can negotiate the best terms and price for the property.

When you are marketing yourself and your services, remember that you should train consumers never to trust the discount agents! Provide increased value to your services and market yourself accordingly. Discount agents have discounted service and discounted marketing. Outshine them with your marketing and services. Take the opportunity to have excellent photography that correctly represents the property, and an excellent social media presence that highlights your brand, vision, and value. Write a rich description and take advantage of every opportunity to let people know you're in the business to sell this home. If you aren't a skilled writer, there is free AI (artificial intelligence) technology available on the internet that can help you draft descriptions, posts, and scripts. Utilize what is at your fingertips! Without marketing you won't sell any homes. You (and the consumer) get what is paid for. Don't go cheap!

Outshine the imitators by relentlessly pushing the boundaries in your systems, procedures, and marketing strategies. Stay several steps ahead of the competition with your quality and consistency. Let everyone know you're in the business, and you'll gain the omnipresence and social media footprint that you need to grow your business.

Chapter 7: Lead Generation & Prospecting

For successful lead generation and prospecting, always be prepared with an answer for people as to why you're the best in the area and how you do things differently than everyone else. Always be client facing and professional since you never know who is watching you. You should be prepared to have an answer ready for how you can provide them service and share your local expertise.

When a lead comes in from your lead sources, statistics show that it is best practice to reach out to them within the first five minutes, otherwise they are more likely to buy or sell with another agent. Normally folks do business with the first person to pick up the phone. Remember that you're not ever selling anything but yourself, so make them trust you and believe in you. Speak with confidence, empathy, and listen. Respond with questions that lead to results. Anticipate their objections and answer them before they arise. This will pattern your speech and conversations toward the close. Keep your focus, discipline and good habits in place to pursue "the close" and tomorrow's business.

We talked previously about the importance of time-blocking and prioritization. You can protect your prospecting time by time blocking the first two hours in the morning with lead generation. No showings or consultations should be scheduled during this time. You can schedule your appointments after you have completed your calls to new leads, circle prospecting around the neighborhood that you have homes listed in, and any for-sale-by-owner prospecting.

You can use this time to send at least 5 handwritten cards, send 5 Facebook messages, make 5 phone calls, and send 5 text messages in addition to your routine lead follow up and generation. This will help you boost your sphere and networking as you market your services and remind folks that you're the best in the business. This is the most significant part of your day.

A good Customer Relationship Management software can also help you stay more efficient with top-of-the-line technology and systems. You can set up drip campaigns where your leads are automatically texted and emailed when they come in. Certain drip campaigns can also set reminders for you to call the lead, with other follow up notes automatically scheduled into your calendar. You can connect your lead sources to your website, and spend extra advertising dollars to boost your reach. Having a good Customer Relationship Management software integrated into the backend of your website and lead capture helps streamline your process for nurturing leads when they come in, and tracking your leads as you prospect. There are several different options for websites, lead integration and CRMs. You can also integrate your local Multiple Listing Service into your website so that leads can search for homes directly on your website.

When you're ready for your buyer's consultations, be sure to arrive early to any meeting with your materials prepared. You should keep a buyer consultation presentation with you - either a hardcopy or a digital one - that can be customized to meet your needs and adjusted for each client. Once you find the client's "why," you can use their "why" to better help them. Sometimes using a cost of waiting report can also help the buyer see the cost of not buying now, depending on the market.

For complete access to a buyer's consultation presentation example, a cost of waiting report template, as well as a list of various CRM and website integration platforms you can use, remember to join our Facebook Group Community by scanning this QR code.

As you build up your team, you want to keep the team as the focus of the conversation with your new clients, and talk up the team for the golden handoff to your administration and transaction coordination after the buyer is under contract. You can also help the buyer get connected with one of your preferred lenders to become pre-approved sooner rather than later so that when an offer is ready to be made, the buyer will already be prepared. It's a good rule of thumb to only show one house to a buyer who is not pre-approved, otherwise it can become a waste of time for everyone. If they can't afford to buy the homes they want to see, then how would it help anyone to spend your valuable time showing them? When they are pre-approved, it's a good practice to put together 3-5 homes to show them, and explain that they won't need to see any more than that since you have found homes that exactly meet their preferences. You can remind them that since they have communicated to you exactly what they want, you've found homes that include all their preferred specifications. Since you've found these homes, is there any reason they shouldn't continue with an offer?

"Tie down" questions at the end of your statements that encourage the client to agree with you will lead the client to the close. Ask strategic questions that compel your prospects to say yes, and you will boost your sales with this technique. Using tie downs, being direct, and keeping good communication will help save everyone time in the long run.

The only exception to scheduling showings after 12pm (so you can maintain your prospecting time in the morning from 9:30-11:30), is if the client works the second or third shift and cannot make an appointment at any other time in the day. You'll want to arrive at least 15 minutes early to the showing or appointment so that you can turn all the lights on, put any toilet seat lids down, and have the MLS sheet with details of the home handy and available for the client.

For your own safety, you should also let your team know where you're going or just put it on your calendar - especially when you're dealing with someone who might make you feel uncomfortable so that others know where you will be. You must generally be aware of your surroundings and always run a quick background check. (A great resource for this is Forewarn, which is a proactive safety and intelligence app for real estate agents that provides instant knowledge prior to face-to-face meetings).

You'll never know what you may find on the property. If you ever feel uncomfortable meeting a client, ask another agent to join you or just refer the client to another agent for a referral fee. Always be better safe than sorry!

Depending on your state and its real estate board requirements, you will want to make sure the client signs and understands the buyer brokerage agreement and explain why an agency agreement is necessary. Here is a fool-proof script to follow: "If you would like me to be available to offer expert advice and guidance, provide detailed information about the properties we see and the ones you have interest in, then the law requires that we sign a Buyer's Agency Agreement form.... This is most beneficial to you and prevents me from just being a door-opener for you, otherwise unable to provide the guidance you may need."

It might help the buyer as you're showing them homes to create notes specifically for them explaining the amenities of the home and why these amenities would be favorable to them. Most of all, your aim is to help them understand how each home meets their "why." What is the property close to? What are the features and benefits of home? Why does it align with their motivation?

When you attach a benefit to each feature of the home, i.e., "This large family room provides space for a growing family so that when...you could have...and a fireplace-so that when...you can have..." etc., it allows the clients to realistically envision their life in the new home. You can also bring a comparative market analysis to have a launching pad for an offer if necessary. When you're showing homes, it is helpful to bring a 25 ft. tape measure and a flashlight since you never know when you'll need them. Clients often want to measure spaces to make sure certain items will fit in the home, and they might want to look in the crawl space or other darker areas of the home that may not have available lighting.

If you're working with a real estate investor, they normally look for an appreciation on a property that is in a good area but also improving. They assess potential cash flow and incoming rents to pay for mortgage, insurance, and taxes to help them finalize if it will be a desirable property. Investors will want vacancies to stay low on investment properties. Discover how to evaluate the profitability of a property using the cap rate. Simply divide the property's net operating income by its value and you'll have a clear picture of its potential yield over one year. You'll also want to make sure you are familiar with the investor's motivation for the property, will they want to buy and hold the property? Flip the property? Use the property as a short-term or long-term rental? This may affect their cash-on-cash return on the investment. So, when you're entering an appointment with a potential investor, you'll want to prepare some notes for them considering these aspects.

We've spent some time discussing buyer's consultations and showings, now let's briefly discuss seller's consultations and listing appointments. As you prepare to meet sellers on listing appointments, you need to take an opportunity to do your research first and make yourself knowledgeable about the area. So be prepared! You can even schedule the presentation at the client's home, and bring a comparative market analysis with you to the listing presentation. Maybe bring examples of your marketing campaigns, or a "Just Listed" postcard example or other published ads in the newspaper that you've run before. Use this appointment to set the seller's expectations and explain the process of a price reduction after the marketing campaigns have successfully run. Pitch your listing price based on the market, and bring the prepared listing paperwork with you. Use this appointment to set the seller's expectations, review your marketing plan and transaction action steps, and handle any possible objections before they arise to save yourself heightened emotions later. You can also provide tips to the seller on preparing their home for professional listing pictures and showings.

For complete access to a seller's listing presentation example and tips for preparing their home for the market, remember to join our Facebook Group Community by scanning this QR code.

In your lead generation and prospecting, it's best to get ahead of the game before meeting potential clients for appointments. Research the area so you can impress them with your knowledge and credibility! Stay consistent with your communication and show them examples of your successful marketing campaigns and extra resources to provide them with an overview of why your services stand out from the rest. Be prepared to wow them with value!

Bad real estate agents are the biggest threat to good real estate agents because they have an unfair advantage in the market. They often undercut prices and provide subpar services, but customers may be more likely to choose them over a legitimate business if they discount their services. If the agent doesn't know or understand their own value, how will the client? This can hurt the reputation of all those involved in the profession, making it difficult for honest employees to make a living and keep up with the competition. To combat this, accountability and experience can be a decisive tool in helping agents stay competitive and learn how to operate a successful real estate business.

A well-functioning agent or team that has the systems and procedures in place, along with high quality leads with the proper scripting and follow up - will allow its agents to build relationships and a better reputation than the poor agents in the business. Accountability and higher quality service will also provide the opportunity to work alongside other established professionals who can provide guidance on everything from marketing strategies and customer relations, maybe even financial management and legal paperwork. Increasing accountability also creates an opportunity to ask questions, receive feedback, and gain practical skills that can help you improve your business and gain valuable experience. Newer team members should strive to show respect, and listen carefully to all advice being offered from more experienced agents. Likewise, an experienced agent should take the time to explain things clearly and understand the unique needs of their surrounding agents and team members.

Bad real estate agents can pose a serious threat to those just starting out or who don't have much experience in the industry, so be wary of any advice given by agents who may be out to make a quick buck, rather than genuinely offering you help. Build or find a good team with accountability, training, and resources to succeed. Afterall, it's all about the customer experience. nsufficient agents without enough experience come into situations and don't give the client what they need. They don't give a high level of integrity. They don't do what they say or say what they'll do. They don't have enough experience. They're not educating themselves. Not reading the newest trends. That's why more attention to follow through needs to be given to the lead follow up and nurture portion of the business. Follow through with what you say you're going to do, and always over deliver. Over communicate. Over serve your client with your level of expertise and team experience.

A capable real estate professional stays on top of lead nurturing and follow up since certain communication can be the difference between a successful sale and lost business. Let's review some tips to create successful follow up and lead nurture campaigns:

Consider setting up automated emails, text messages, or even phone calls with lead nurturing content that will help you stay connected to potential clients without taking too much of your time. Automating your follow up process is an efficient way to ensure leads don't slip through the cracks. For effective lead nurturing, you'll want to focus on providing relevant and targeted content. Consider creating content adapted to a buyer's needs, such as market trends in a particular area or home-buying tips. Your goal should be to show potential buyers that you value them by personalizing your communications. Include their name, address the individual directly, and ask questions about what they're looking for in a home. This will help build trust and show that you take the time to learn about them. Just don't forget to stay in touch with potential buyers even after they purchase a home. Keep your clients informed on new listings, price changes, and other market news that could be relevant to them.

You can also leverage the power of social media to reach potential buyers. Posting home listings, helpful tips, and connecting with buyers on social platforms can help you maintain contact with leads while also providing value.

Investing in marketing resources is another great way to create lead nurturing content and stay connected with potential buyers. Be resourceful and take the time to research the latest trends in real estate. You can use analytics to gain insights into your target market, and consider investing in software or other digital tools that could facilitate an efficient lead nurturing process. Sharing your knowledge can be a solid way to build relationships with potential buyers, spread awareness of your business, and create a positive reputation in the industry. Plus, you'll gain valuable insight as you teach and learn from others in the field. You can consider helping other real estate professionals by hosting mastermind groups with them about lead generation and lead nurturing.

Take action on your lead nurturing goals. Make sure you are regularly reaching out to leads, following up on inquiries, and providing helpful information that could be useful for future buyers. Staying organized with a designated lead tracking system can help you stay on top of each step in the process. With consistent effort and determination, you'll be able to make meaningful connections with potential buyers that will lead to increased appointments.

Building relationships with leads should be a priority throughout the lead nurturing process. Take time to get to know leads on an individual level, and find ways to provide value beyond just your services as a real estate agent. By investing in your relationships, you will create trust and loyalty between yourself and potential buyers.

Asking for feedback is also a great way to gain valuable insights into your lead nurturing process. Ask clients about their experiences, how you could improve your services, and what type of content they would like to receive in the future. By implementing feedback from leads, you may be able to increase conversions and sales in the long-term. As with any sound business strategy, regularly evaluate your lead nurturing process to make sure it is still meeting your objectives. Revisit your goals and metrics on a regular basis to see what areas need improvement. Consider experimenting with different tactics that could potentially produce better results and stay open-minded about new approaches so that you can ensure your lead nurturing process is always working in top form.

Don't forget that lead nurturing takes patience and persistence. You may need to reach out multiple times before leads are ready to take the next step. By being consistent and making sure to never miss an opportunity for connection, you will be able to create lasting relationships with potential buyers.

If you are on a team, leverage the team's leads and follow up systems. The team will always help you more than you help the team so take advantage of its accountability, incoming leads, and follow up systems to build your business as you work toward leading your own team and growing as a real estate agent.

If you are not on a team, I encourage you to join our Facebook group community to get involved with other entrepreneurs like yourself who are serious about becoming top-producers in their markets. Here you will gain access to accountability, resources, and opportunities for further training.

For complete access to various scripts, email templates, drip campaigns, and other resources for lead nurturing and follow up, join our Facebook group community by scanning this QR code.

Are you looking for ways to increase your productivity as a real estate agent? The best way is to review your operations process, and focus on task-oriented activities instead of "busy work." Busy work can waste precious time and resources, so focus on tasks that will actually move the needle in your business. Instead of spending too much time on administrative tasks or other non-essential activities first in your day, you should focus your prime energy on marketing, networking, and research that will result in tangible production outcomes. With these as the priority, then you can fit in your other administrative tasks and non-essential activities later in your day. When you start feeling yourself getting behind on these tasks weekly, then you can begin to hire out help with the administrative and "busy work" side of the business as leverage for your production to continue.

To execute your essential activities, you'll need to set your schedule and stick to it. It's easy to get sidetracked when you don't have a plan of attack. Make sure that your daily tasks are mapped out ahead of time, and don't be afraid to set aside some "flex" for yourself as well in between some tasks to allow time to catch up. "Flex" time can be used to change gears and jump ahead to some administrative tasks, or this could look like 15 minutes to run through emails, texts, or calls missed while you were working in your other time-blocks. You could also use "flex" time for a mental break, those are important too! When you have a plan, it makes it much easier to stay productive and on track.

If you find yourself overwhelmed by the thought of tackling a big appointment or making your calls, make sure to break the big task down into smaller pieces that are easier for you to manage. The more steps you can take towards your end goal, the closer you'll be to achieving success. If you are on a team, you can also delegate certain tasks among your team members if need be.

Deadlines are also fundamental for staying on track, as long as they are reasonable due dates that you can actually meet. If you give yourself too tight of a timeline, you may end up feeling overwhelmed and frustrated when you miss the mark.

Give yourself time to recharge and refocus. Step away from your computer screen every now and then to reset your brain since burnout is one of the biggest productivity killers. It can be helpful to build in small refreshers to keep your mental focus.

You can also find an accountability partner that you can report your progress to as a great way to stay motivated and on task. If you have someone that's holding you accountable, it will be much easier to stay focused and reach your goals. It's also hard to be productive when you don't have the right tools or resources.

Invest in yourself by purchasing the necessary equipment, attending seminars or webinars, and taking the time to learn new skills or techniques. These investments will pay off in the long run by helping you to become a more distinctive real estate agent and business owner. It's difficult to be productive in a negative atmosphere or amid pessimistic people. Spend time with people who are encouraging and uplifting, this will naturally help increase your motivation. Surrounding yourself with individuals who have similar goals or ambitions can help keep you inspired and focused on your work.

Remember to join our Facebook Group community by scanning the QR code to surround yourself with a community of other real estate professionals who are on this journey together.

You need to make sure that as you grow in your business and build your team, that the team has the right people in the right positions. That each person understands their highest dollar producing activity. Then they can also focus on that one thing that makes the most money for the team within their position. A man that chases many rabbits never catches any. Narrow your focus and that of your team's on specific tasks, and more will get done in the long run.

It is best practice to constantly improve existing systems and procedures as well as assist others with business development. Doing so facilitates innovation and provides an opportunity to exercise creativity while helping the team reach the desired outcome more quickly. Staying streamlined is not only beneficial professionally but personally too; it promotes growth while improving organization and discipline. Ultimately, staying productive by making wise use of available resources paves the way for success both at work as well as in everyday life. Remember, there's a difference between activity and action. Action targeted in the right direction moves the business forward, while mindless activity can keep the business stale. So don't be busy, be productive in your operations. The team's operations feed into all other activities. When the life blood runs clean, so will the other parts of the business.

Operations can also help you keep the divisions of the business running smoothly - from bookkeeping and reporting, to contracts and listings, training, client care, marketing and event planning. All of these divisions are significant, but learning how to organize your schedule to include each category is even more significant. When it is just you as the solo-agent building your brand, you need to make time for each of these divisions of operations that move the business forward. Using a time-block scheduling approach is a great way to ensure that you are committing time in your schedule to each of these demands. Then as you grow and hire an administrator to help you with some operations tasks, you will be able to delegate to leverage the highest and best use of your time.

For complete access to instructions on how to build a foolproof operation manual, job descriptions, time-block schedule, and an organizational task chart to keep your real estate business moving forward, join our Facebook Group community by scanning this QR code.

You can also use meeting templates to keep meetings short and concise, and you can use checklists or follow an operation manual to make sure that the daily, weekly, quarterly, and yearly tasks are being completed for each division of business. To access the templates that our team uses for Weekly Meeting Agendas, and various daily, weekly, monthly, quarterly, and annual Checklists for the divisions of business, you can join our Facebook page and engage in a community of others who are growing with you.

CHAPTER 10: TRAINING & EDUCATION

The real estate industry requires hard work and training in order to succeed, but it is a great way to generally learn how to be a student of life. Training opportunities for the team leader and team members can not only help increase systems and procedures - but also their experience. In house administration (not virtual assistance) that manages contracts to closings also requires consistent training in changing laws, documents, and updating processes. As long as you stay focused and determined in your own training and in providing applicable training to your team members, you can help your administrators create a successful career for themselves in the industry as well.

Training and education require active listening. Listening with the intention of learning can be a challenging exercise, but one that yields great dividends. By actively listening, we allow ourselves to take in more than just words and comprehend their true meaning. Doing this allows us to gain a greater understanding of what is being said and fills in any gaps which may exist from a lack of knowledge or experience. Learning through listening helps us go beyond what we already know by allowing room for new perspectives to build our skills. A conscious effort needs to be made when listening to better understand the ideas and make sure all the basic concepts are clear. It takes focus, discipline and an open-mind. But ultimately provides us with more interesting ways of viewing things and enables us to have meaningful conversations so we can make cecisions faster with clearer considerations.

Don't listen for the answer you want to hear - listen for the truth. God gave us two ears and one mouth for a reason, so that we can listen with the intention of learning. Listen to improve. And then ask great questions for a well-informed response.

You can also network with other professionals in the industry and reach out to established investors, brokers, and agents who can help you navigate the real estate market.

Being able to adjust quickly to changing markets and technologies will give you an edge over your competition, so take the time to educate yourself. Get an understanding of the local market, research trends in housing prices, and stay up-to-date on business news.

When you set goals that are both short-term and long-term you can hone in on the training necessary to achieve these goals and establish a clear strategy to accomplish them.

You can take courses and seminars to stay current on the latest real estate trends to invest in yourself so that you can improve your skill set. You can also utilize technology in your training and education to enhance your services and skill set.

Remember that success takes time. Persistence and dedication are key elements in becoming a successful real estate agent, so don't give up when times get tough; instead, use those experiences as an opportunity to learn and grow. Take time to read books on real estate from all those experts who have gone before you to gain a better understanding of the industry and how to best approach it.

Learning does not have to be confined to the classroom or office space. Education comes from experience, so don't be afraid to take risks and gain first-hand knowledge. Take what you have learned and use it as leverage when setting goals for yourself. Establishing both short and long-term objectives can help keep you motivated, organized, and inspired even during the toughest of times. Make sure to establish realistic goals and commit to them.

Use any available resources around you to help stay on top of your game. Keeping up with various mediums such as podcasts or webinars can help you stay informed and in-the-know. Additionally, participating in real estate masterminds or attending local conferences is a great way to network with other professionals in the industry and learn from their experiences. So don't be afraid to get out there and start networking! Remember, training and education all boils down to dedication. The road to success won't always be easy, but with hard work and dedication you can push yourself to greater limits than your competitors.

For a list of books and training resources, real estate coaching programs, and other helpful classes to enhance your real estate career, join our Facebook Group community by scanning this QR code.

PART 3 - TOP OF THE FUNNEL

Once your mindset and general systems and procedures have been established, this stage of the funnel represents your clientele's journey through your resources, scripts, advertising, and prospecting more in detail to make sure that you are exhibiting top-notch lead follow-up and marketing for the business. Every item coming into your real estate business must be filtered through your communication, which builds your reputation. You can communicate through your lead nurturing - as well as your marketing and advertising - to provide value to others and build your brand.

Chapter 11 - Edu-Tainment

Edu-tainment is material that blends education and entertainment at the same time. Having a strong brand voice is a necessity for any successful real estate expert, since you must be able to communicate excellently with your customers, investors, and potential partners in order to build relationships and grow your business.

To create an operational brand voice that will help you stand out from the competition and make sure that you are successfully marketing yourself to the right audience, you will need to know your audience. Before you begin, ask yourself who you are targeting with your brand voice. Are you targeting potential buyers or sellers? Are they first-time homebuyers or experienced real estate investors? Identifying this target market will help ensure that your message resonates with and reaches the right people.

Then you need to define your brand values, or obtain clarity on the team's brand values. Understanding what sets you apart from others in the real estate market is key to creating a unique and powerful brand voice. Defining your core values and mission statement will help shape the language that you use when communicating with potential customers or partners.

Relevant content to your target audience is the essence of successful marketing campaigns. This content could include blog posts, videos, podcasts, social media graphics, or other forms of content that will reach your desired demographic. Identify trends in the real estate market and use these to inform the focus of your content.

Don't be afraid to interact with your followers. Whether through comments, DMs, or emails, responding to questions and engaging with those who have an interest in your brand will help build trust and grow relationships. To make sure your brand voice remains relevant in the real estate market, stay active on social media and other channels. Keep track of industry trends and be sure to post regularly in order to keep your followers engaged.

Collaborating with other professionals or businesses that are related to the real estate market can also be a great way to enhance your brand voice and reach new potential customers. Consider partnering with local businesses, industry publications, or related organizations who can help you extend your reach. Collaboration over competition in the real estate world is a great way to advertise together, educate together, and provide value together.

Keep your "edu-tainment" valid, relevant, short and engaging to keep it fun for others to watch. Real estate isn't a fun business, it can be boring. All the more reason to make your content eye-catching and different, silly and unique to provide an edge over your competitors. The more stories you can tell through your content, the more applicable and measurable it will be to your clients.

For resources on how to create a hook, story, or offer with your real estate video content that entertains and informs others with your brand voice, join our Facebook Group Community by scanning this QR Code.

CHAPTER 12 - SCRIPTS & OBJECTION HANDLING

It's easy to become a real estate agent but hard to become a successful one. Many agents lack the knowledge on beneficial objection handling, and don't practice their scripts on negotiation. Training changes everything. It changes your scripts, confidence, and systems and procedures. The current fail rate of an average agent is 87% in the first 2 years, and that doesn't count part time agents. Becoming a real estate agent is not hard - but being a successful agent is difficult. Normally an agent needs to prepare 5-6 months of savings in their bank account to help them as they get started before they have their first closing. But agents on a team tend to close their first 2-9 deals in their first 90 days. This shows the difference a team can have on the success of new agents especially, as it provides the training and support that they need.

Expert negotiation allows agents to better protect the clients and ensure a smooth transaction. Handling any objection or conflict can normally be preemptively avoided with good expectations set at the beginning of the transaction, and good communication maintained throughout.

Listening to your client's motive will also help you with scripting your conversations and handling objections as they arise. What if the highest price isn't the best offer if the sellers need temporary occupancy post-closing? It is best to know their motive so that you can capitalize on what would be most beneficial for both parties as objections arise, and pay special attention any time that clients are willing to forgo a bit on the purchase price for something else in their best interest.

For any conflict resolution or objection that arises, before even responding you should listen carefully and ask questions to understand the situation better. Once you have heard and understood the objection, provide relevant facts and figures to support your position. Reassure clients that their concerns are taken seriously and be confident in your responses. Clients need to know that they can trust you and your expertise in order to make informed decisions about their real estate transaction. Let them know that you are confident in your ability to handle any objections they may have. One of the most applicable tools for objection handling is simply listening to what your clients have to say. Taking time to really hear their objections and understand them will help you come up with a mutually beneficial solution. Listening to your client's objections and understanding their perspective will help you craft a tailored solution that addresses their concerns. Making sure to actively listen to their points of view and ask follow up questions can also help you better understand the motivations behind their position, allowing you to come up with more worthwhile solutions.

When you agree, align, and ask questions to your clients during this process, it guides the objection handling and conversation to a more positive level.

AGREE: I hear you...

ALIGN: You are not alone...

ASK: Ask a question to frame the conversation in the direction you need it to go...

Example: I completely understand! I have been in a similar situation *or* I have had clients who felt the same way. Can I ask you a question? *Now this is your chance to frame the conversation.*

Clients may feel overwhelmed with real estate transactions, and you have the opportunity to show them empathy and understanding. You'll also want to be mindful of any cultural and language differences throughout the transaction. Reassuring clients that their concerns are valid and taking ownership of any mistakes can help to boost their confidence in you. Make sure to stay in constant communication with your client throughout the process to make sure that any issues are resolved in a timely manner, and resist the urge to rush your client or pressure them into an agreement.

Always have a plan of action to present and be prepared to negotiate, if necessary, so that you continue to offer solutions. Make sure to record all conversations that take place during a real estate transaction as this can help with dispute resclution in the future. Keep track of all the details during the negotiation process, including any objections that have been raised and the solutions that have been proposed. This will help ensure that you can refer back to them later if needed, and provide an accurate record of your transactions. Once you have addressed an objection, you'll want to follow-up with clients to ensure they are satisfied with how the issue was resolved. This ensures that all parties involved are on the same page and that any solutions proposed have been addressed. This shows that you take the clients' needs seriously and value their feedback. Seeking advice from experienced professionals who have been through similar situations can also help you gain valuable insight and stay focused on the goal of reaching an agreement with your client.

It's also helpful to stay up-to-date with the latest industry trends, market conditions, and other related topics so that you can confidently address any potential issues that may arise during the transaction. If an objection is not being resolved, it may be best to end the conversation and look for a solution at another time. Gently suggest solutions and help clients consider alternatives that might be better suited for their needs.

If you feel that an objection is becoming too difficult to handle, don't be afraid to reach out to colleagues or a business mentor for advice. Having a support network can make all the difference when it comes to successfully navigating objections from your clients. Keeping a positive attitude throughout the transaction will help ensure that both parties remain professional and amicable towards one another, resulting in smoother negotiations and better outcomes for everyone.

Knowing beforehand what objections your clients may have can help you be better equipped to handle them when they arise. Preparation always goes a long way in helping ycu understand the needs of your clients and providing the best service possible. Just remember that the purpose of objection handling is to reach an agreement that is beneficial to both you and your client. Keep this goal in mind will help you stay focused on the task at hand and prevent the conversation from veering off course.

As with any skill, objection handling takes time and practice to hone. Taking every opportunity to practice your craft will help you become more efficient and better prepared to handle any objections that come your way. Objection handling should be done in a professional manner, making sure to remain respectful at all times. This will help ensure that clients feel comfortable raising their objections and trust you with finding the best resolution for them.

Keeping your client informed of any changes or potential issues that may arise throughout the transaction can also help prevent common objections from cropping up in the first place. Making sure to communicate with them regularly and take preventive measures will ensure a smoother real estate transaction for all parties involved. Even when faced with the toughest objections, having a positive attitude can go far in resolving any roadblocks quickly and cordially. Your goal is to help your client find an agreement that works for everyone - so approach each objection with a smile and a can-do attitude!

As with any dispute resolution process, remain open-minded and flexible when handling objections. Try to keep an open dialogue with your clients and assess all potential solutions before coming to a decision. By taking the time to listen to their thoughts and ideas, you can often come up with creative solutions that everyone can agree on.

If you want to avoid misunderstandings with your clients, make sure to communicate clearly about the process. Explain the steps you'll take to address their concerns, and provide updates on progress as needed. This will help to ensure that everyone is on the same page and prevent any unnecessary delays or confusion. Remember - no matter how difficult the situation becomes, stay professional at all times. Resist the urge to become defensive or confrontational, and instead focus on providing a resolution that both parties can accept. This will help to maintain a positive relationship with your clients, and ensure that everyone is satisfied in the end.

Objection handling can often feel like an uphill battle so it is best to establish trust early on with your clients. Listening is a fundamental part of any successful negotiation. When you give your clients the time and attention they deserve, you ensure that their concerns are heard and taken seriously. When you receive an objection, take your time to dig deeper into the issue and understand it from all angles before offering a solution. Respond to objections in a timely manner to show that you respect your clients and value their feedback, and to provide clear and concise updates on the progress of the transaction so that everyone stays on track.

Always offer viable solutions or alternatives that can practically address objections. This will demonstrate your commitment towards finding a satisfactory solution for all parties involved. If the objections are not addressed in a satisfactory manner, see if there's room for compromise and adjust your approach accordingly. Be flexible and make any necessary changes to ensure that everyone is happy with the outcome. Always follow up after handling objections in order to ensure that your clients are satisfied with the outcome. Seeing how their concerns were addressed will help build trust and cement your relationship moving forward.

For more tips on objection handling and scripts that can be helpful amidst conflict, join our Facebook Group community by scanning this QR code.

Chapter 13 - Working & Growing Your Sphere

Sometimes growing your sphere is like sifting through a pan of dirt when mining for gold, you have to shake through it all to find a little bit of gold. This prospecting mindset is a critical part of successful real estate. Just like prospectors pan for gold, you need to be on the lookout for opportunities that can bring success and growth in your business. You can stay ahead of the competition and maximize your profits by implementing massive actions that will catch more gold.

Prospecting can be a tedious process. You can stay motivated by taking time to celebrate your successes as they come, and learning from your mistakes. Establish strong relationships, attend events, join networking groups, and introduce yourself to potential clients and partners. Don't wait for things to happen; go out and make them happen! Take initiative and stay on top of the market trends so you can spot potential opportunities early on. You can subscribe to newsletters, listen to podcasts, and attend conferences to stay informed about the industry. By keeping up with current events, you can be sure that your prospects are also well-informed.

Organization is key when it comes to prospecting. You'll need to create a system (or utilize your existing customer relationship management system) to track all of your leads and follow up regularly to ensure nothing and no one slips through the cracks. Diversify your portfolio to minimize risk and increase your chances of success. You can consider different strategies such as flipping, wholesaling, and rental properties, as well as different lead sources.

When you're comparing lead sources, you'll want to focus on finding high quality leads rather than a large volume of low-quality leads. High quality leads will be more likely to convert into sales and maximize your profits. And be patient: real estate prospecting doesn't happen overnight. It may take some time to build relationships and find the right leads.

Networking is a cardinal part of prospecting, so you'll want to join online real estate groups to meet potential leads and grow your business. Technology can be a great asset for real estate networking and prospecting. There are plenty of tools and software that can help you automate tasks, keep track of leads, and generate more business. Consider investing in some of these technologies to increase your efficiency and streamline your process.

For a full list of technological resources, lead sources, and networking groups, join our Facebook group community by scanning this QR code.

Be persistent. Don't give up if you don't get a response right away. Follow up with leads regularly and keep trying until you get the results you want. One of the weightiest parts of prospecting is building relationships with potential customers, so take the time to get to know them and find out what their needs are, so that you can provide the best service possible.

Setting goals is a substantial part of prospecting, as it will give you something to strive for and help keep you motivated. Make sure that your prospecting goals are realistic and achievable for them to serve as a realistic guide as you progress.

CHAPTER 14 - THE IMPORTANCE OF BUILDING YOUR LIST BY COLD-CALLING AND CIRCLE PROSPECTING

There is always more that can be done. More eyes to see the property, more calls that could be made, more advertising that could be blasted, more prospecting and more leads. As a newly licensed realtor or an experienced one, it sets the tone for your career when you continue sharpening your sword and increasing your focus to create massive actions. Obtain the education you are required to have, and then some. Take extra classes to increase your marketing skills. Answer the phone for more opportunities with leads. Create more accountability to your schedule - or there will be many deals that may fall through the cracks without proper accountability or training in place.

Build your list by cold-calling and circle prospecting to get as many feet through the property as you can in order to obtain better and stronger offers. The easiest way to do this is to nurture and grow your sphere of influence, and dial more calls to "For Sale by Owners" and homes near to your subject property. You can use platforms like Mojo dialer to help with this, or other dialers that will connect to your CRM (customer relationship management software).

Your sphere of influence (SOI) consists of people who know you and are willing to refer business to you. These can be friends, family, past clients, or anyone in your network from church, school, etc. Your sphere of influence is a crucial component of your real estate business, making them more likely to work with you or recommend you to others. Building a strong sphere of influence allows you to tap into a reliable source of potential clients and referrals, helping you grow your business. The key to growing your sphere of influence is building genuine relationships with people. This means going beyond just networking and truly getting to know the individuals in your network. Take an interest in their lives, stay in touch, and be a valuable resource for them. Remember, there is always more that can be done. More value that can be given. More genuine relationships that can be built.

Leverage your social media platforms like LinkedIn, Instagram, and Facebook as powerful tools to expand your sphere of influence. Use these platforms to connect with new people, share valuable content, and stay top-of-mind with your existing network. You can also use these platforms to collaborate with other professionals such as mortgage brokers, home inspectors, and attorneys who can help you tap into their network and expand your own. These actions build mutually beneficial relationships that can lead to referrals and partnerships.

You can also get involved in your local community by volunteering, joining committees or organizations, and attending community events. This not only allows you to give back but also helps you build relationships with people in your area.

To truly stand out and be memorable, offer value to your sphere of influence. This could be in the form of helpful resources, informative newsletters, or even just checking in to see how they are doing. By consistently providing value, you will become a trusted and valuable resource for your network. Remember, it's not enough to simply meet people and add them to your sphere of influence. Follow up and stay in touch with them. Maintain relationships and top-of-mind with regular phone calls, emails, or in-person meetings.

In today's digital age, having a strong online presence is principal for expanding your sphere of influence. This includes having a professional website, being active on social media, and utilizing online marketing tactics. By making yourself easily accessible online, you can reach a wider audience and attract potential clients. Another great way to grow your sphere of influence, as I've mentioned, is to attend conferences and seminars related to the real estate industry. These events allow you to network with other professionals, learn new strategies and techniques, and expand your knowledge in the field.

Be genuine and authentic in your interactions with your sphere of influence. People can sense insincerity and it can damage your relationships. Show a genuine interest in others, listen actively, and always follow through on any promises or commitments you make. Don't make everything about your business, but ask first how you can support others in their own business and with their own goals.

By consistently providing value, staying in touch with your network, building your online presence, attending events and being genuine in your interactions, you can expand your sphere of influence and ultimately grow your business. Remember to prioritize relationships and never underestimate the power of networking in the real estate world.

Building these people-skills will also help you host open houses. As a new real estate agent, hosting open houses is a major part of your job. It gives you the opportunity to showcase properties and connect with potential buyers. However, it can also be a daunting task if you are new to the industry. So, to help you successfully host open houses, here are some tips and tricks to keep in mind.

A few days before the open house, you'll want to make sure to call your sphere and other leads within that subject property's price point to make them aware of the open house. Then begin advertising on social media and create an event on Facebook to make it easier to invite people. Run an email campaign and circle-prospect by calling the neighborhood and surrounding area making them aware of the event. Make sure to put signs out, balloons if you want to, and remind all interested leads before the event. Utilize social media, email marketing, and other forms of advertising to promote the open house and attract potential buyers. You can even door-knock the neighborhood 30 minutes or 1 hour before the event to remind neighbors that it will be happening. When you arrive, thoroughly clean and declutter the property if necessary. This will create a good first impression for potential buyers.

Inside the home, you'll need to create a welcoming atmosphere. Make sure to greet visitors with a warm and friendly attitude. This will make them feel more comfortable and encourage them to explore the property. Familiarize yourself with all aspects of the property, including its features, amenities, and history. This will help you answer any questions potential buyers may have. You should also prepare brochures or flyers with information about the property to give out to interested buyers. Potential buyers may have a lot of questions about the property, so be ready to provide them with answers. If you don't know the answer, offer to find out and follow up after the open house. You'll want to have a check-in sheet for any viewers that obtains their name, contact information, and whether or not they're currently working with a real estate agent; this will help you create follow-up opportunities with the potential buyers.

After the open house, input your new contacts into your CRM and follow up with potential buyers who showed interest in the property. This will show that you are dedicated and proactive in helping them find their dream home. As a new real estate agent, hosting open houses will be a learning experience. You can even write thank you cards to the neighbors and thank them for allowing you to invite folks to tour their neighborhood. You can continue to call all new contacts with an update on how the event went, include an offer update on the listing, make yourself available for questions, or just offer assistance to anyone they might know interested in selling. The seller will also need to be updated on the event's turnout or marketing details even if no one ended up coming. Frame all marketing as a win to spread the word of the property's availability. Take note of what worked well and what didn't, and continuously improve for future open houses.

Remember to always maintain a professional demeanor and be enthusiastic about the property. Hosting open houses is a great way to showcase your skills as a real estate agent and build relationships with potential buyers. Keep in mind that hosting open houses is not just about selling a property, but also about building relationships and establishing yourself as a reliable and knowledgeable real estate agent in the industry. So, make sure to always be professional, informative, and personable during open house events. And most importantly, have fun and enjoy the process!

Don't be discouraged if not all open houses lead to immediate sales. Hosting open houses is just one aspect of your overall marketing strategy and it takes time and effort to see results. The more open houses you host, the more exposure you give to properties and the higher chances of connecting with potential buyers. So don't shy away from this aspect of your job, embrace it and make the most out of every open house opportunity.

For a comprehensive checklist of open house preparation and access to a customizable sign-in sheet for your guests, join our Facebook Group by scanning this QR code.

CHAPTER 15 - VELCRO PROSPECTING TO SUSTAIN AND MAINTAIN

There are two main reasons real estate agents don't reach their full potential. When they fall in love with the idea that a little bit of action can cause a little bit of success - they forget that what got them "here" doesn't get them "there." What gained a little bit of success will always plateau, and will not help them break through the glass ceiling to the next level. They don't commit to increasing their actions to increase their results. Then, they do not reinvest their money when they taste a little bit of success. Don't fall prey to these two roadblocks! Instead, a wise real estate agent should put resources back into their business to create more leverage and never settle into complacency.

Especially when it comes to prospecting, remember that what got you where you are won't get you to the next level. Increase your actions, and you'll increase your results. Stay consistent and disciplined - and your hard work will continue to beat even the talent from those around you. Send more handwritten letters, send more emails, call more leads. Doing a little bit more everyday will help you reach your goals.

As a new real estate agent, one of the biggest challenges you may face is generating leads and finding potential clients. You need to have a clear understanding of your target market. This means identifying the specific demographics and geographical areas that are most likely to be interested in buying or selling real estate so that you can match your prospecting efforts to reach the right audience.

Referrals are also a powerful source of leads for real estate agents. When satisfied clients refer their friends and family to you, it not only brings in new business, but it also builds trust and credibility. Make sure to provide exceptional service and ask for referrals from happy clients. Even character reviews are helpful from your sphere of influence when you're first becoming established as a new professional.

There are numerous online tools specifically designed for lead generation in the real estate industry. These can include lead capture forms on your website, landing pages for targeted campaigns, and lead management software. Utilizing these tools can help streamline your lead generation process and make it more efficient. Make sure to contact these leads with calls, texts, and emails in their first seven days of entering your database so that you can remain top-of-mind when they are beginning their search. Always seek to set the appointment with them so that you can close the deal. This is always best done in person so that you can read their body language, connect with them on a deeper level and align with them.

For examples of landing pages for targeted campaigns, lead capture forms, and "seven days of pain" scripts for new leads, join our Facebook group by scanning this QR code.

PART 4 - MIDDLE OF THE FUNNEL

Once you have transformed your clientele to "stick" to you, the next stage of the funnel teaches you how to negotiate on their behalf, increase the quality of your service, and re-engage your clients and sphere to remain top-of-mind. As incoming business flows down the funnel, it must be filtered through the best quality and highest level of service to transform its chemical makeup into long-lasting client retention and name you as the local expert.

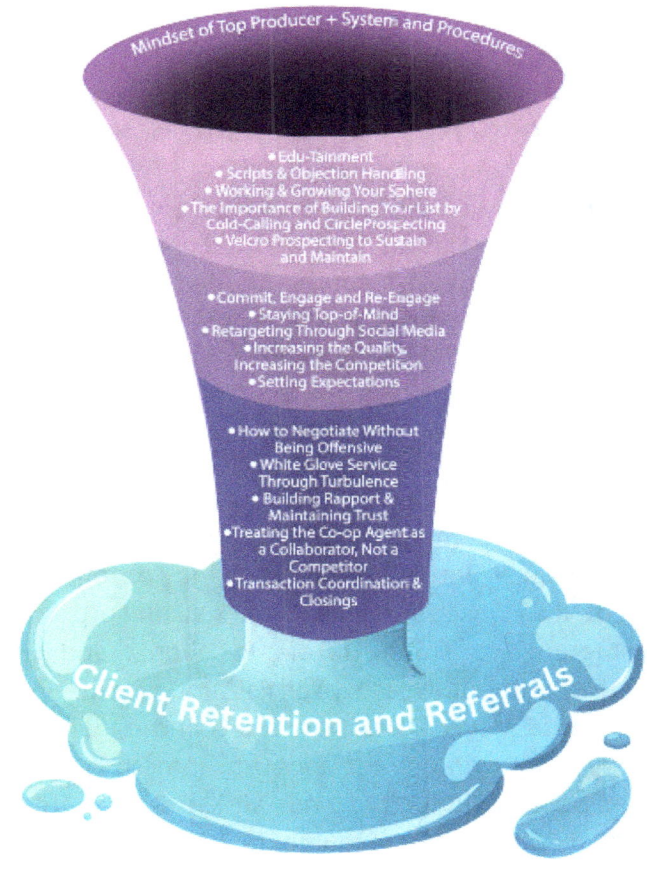

Mindset of Top Producer + Systems and Procedures

- Edu-Tainment
- Scripts & Objection Handling
- Working & Growing Your Sphere
- The Importance of Building Your List by Cold-Calling and CircleProspecting
- Velcro Prospecting to Sustain and Maintain

- Commit, Engage and Re-Engage
- Staying Top-of-Mind
- Retargeting Through Social Media
- Increasing the Quality, Increasing the Competition
- Setting Expectations

- How to Negotiate Without Being Offensive
- White Glove Service Through Turbulence
- Building Rapport & Maintaining Trust
- Treating the Co-op Agent as a Collaborator, Not a Competitor
- Transaction Coordination & Closings

Client Retention and Referrals

Chapter 16 - Commit, Engage and Re-Engage

When people lack commitment, they lose opportunities and they are less likely to reach their goals. All you have to do is commit and engage your leads by doing more than the other percentage of real estate agents who lack commitment. A great way to maintain your commitment is by constantly engaging with your leads and building strong relationships with them to ultimately close more deals.

Sometimes leads may lose interest or become unresponsive after initial contact. It is imperative for you to have creative strategies to re-engage these leads and keep them interested in your services. One of the most noteworthy aspects of engaging with leads is building personalized connections. This means taking the time to really get to know your leads on an individual level and designing your communication and approach accordingly. This can include sending personalized emails, handwritten notes, or even small gifts to show that you value their business and appreciate them as individuals. Remembering birthdays or home anniversaries, and sending personalized video messages on those days will show that you value your leads as individuals and are willing to go the extra mile for them.

I can't emphasize enough that social media is a powerful tool for engaging with leads and staying top-of-mind. As a real estate agent, it is consequential to have a strong presence on platforms like Instagram, YouTube, TikTok, Facebook, and LinkedIn. Use these platforms to showcase your listings, provide valuable insights and tips about the real estate market, and engage with your followers. Everything from market updates, home buying and selling tips, and even posts on industry trends and strategies. By positioning yourself as a knowledgeable resource, leads will see you as a trusted advisor and be more likely to reach out to you when they are ready to make a move.

Hosting events is another great way to engage with leads in person and create a memorable experience. These events can range from small gatherings like wine tastings or cooking classes, to larger events such as open houses or charity fundraisers. This gives you the opportunity to connect with leads in a more relaxed setting and showcase your expertise and personality.

The most sustainable way to engage and re-engage leads is to provide more valuable and relevant content than any of your competitors. This content includes blog posts, daily videos, webinars, or weekly newsletters. By sharing useful and relevant information, you position yourself as a trained and trusted resource in the real estate industry. This will not only help keep your leads engaged, but also attract new ones through word-of-mouth referrals.

Sometimes leads need an extra push to take action, and offering incentives can be just the thing to re-engage them. These incentives can include giveaway prizes or even appropriate gifts from partnering businesses such as home renovation companies or moving companies. (Just make sure you follow your state's guidelines on appropriate gift-giving policies in place from the Real Estate Board). These types of offers can be promoted through social media, email campaigns, and at events.

So, with personalized communication, valuable and relevant social media content, client events and offering incentives like giveaway prizes or gifts from partnering businesses, you can reignite their interest. Get your leads to take action with a little extra motivation and even the most hesitant prospects will be re-engaged.

CHAPTER 17 - STAYING TOP-OF-MIND

If agents are not consistent with their follow up campaigns, then their sphere will forget they are in the industry and may use someone else when the time comes for them to buy or sell. Follow up every step of the way. Staying top of mind with your clients and prospects is a prerequisite for building a successful business. It means being the first person they think of when they have any real estate needs or know someone who does.

Stay ahead of the competition in a fast-paced industry by being proactive and maintaining visibility. By doing so, you open doors for providing value and staying connected. Invest in your brand to stand out among other real estate agents. Your brand is your unique selling point and leaves a lasting impression. Create a strong and consistent brand that aligns with your values and personality. Have a professional logo, website, social media presence, business card, and other marketing materials.

Be proactive in your outreach efforts by connecting with past clients and offering them a free-market analysis or just a check-in to see how they are doing. Offer valuable insights and advice, and let them know that you are always available to help with any real estate needs they may have.

Maximize your success as a real estate agent in your local community by being actively involved and visible. Sponsoring local events, volunteering, or joining community organizations are all possible ways to build relationships and increase brand recognition. However, it doesn't stop there. Stay top of mind with your clients by consistently providing value and expertise. Share branded market updates, neighborhood insights, and helpful tips for buying or selling properties. By positioning yourself as an expert and trusted advisor and connecting your content to your unique brand, you'll be the first person that clients think of when they need real estate services.

Stay connected with your clients and prospects beyond the initial transaction through follow-up emails, phone calls, social media interactions, or even just sending them a quick note on their birthday or anniversary. When you maintain a genuine relationship with your clients, they will be more likely to remember you, your brand, and refer you to others.

You can also use email marketing to send out newsletters or updates on the real estate market. And when you invest in a reliable customer relationship management (CRM) system to keep track of your clients and prospects and stay in touch with them regularly, you can expand your platform to showcase your listings, share valuable content, and engage with your audience.

Remember, go above and beyond in terms of communication, responsiveness, and attention to detail in all your interactions with your clients. Happy clients are more likely to refer you to their friends and family, keeping you top of mind with potential clients. Like I mentioned, don't forget to keep in touch with your clients even after the transaction is complete. This shows that you care about their well-being and are genuinely interested in maintaining a relationship with them.

Offer value beyond just buying and selling homes. You can provide branded resources for home maintenance or improvement, connect clients with trusted professionals in your network, or host educational seminars on topics related to real estate. By offering valuable insights and branding your services, you position yourself as a knowledgeable and reliable resource, keeping you top of mind with clients. As the saying goes, "out of sight, out of mind." Make an effort to attend networking events in your community to meet new people and reconnect with past clients. This allows you to expand your network and stay connected with potential leads. Don't forget to bring business cards and make personal connections by following up with individuals after the event.

Chapter 18 - Retargeting Through Social Media

Retargeting your audience using social media requires you to articulate your ad campaigns to target behavior patterns, interests, demographics, and geographic locations. You should do a little research beforehand and use platforms like Witly or Facebook Business Pages to run your specific ad campaigns. You can also use Google Ad words to create Google or other Local Services campaigns that will obtain more pay per click or pay per call leads. Retargeting audiences through social media also involves using targeted ads to reach potential clients who may not already be following you on social media. Facebook and Instagram offer advanced targeting options that allow you to select specific demographics, interests, and behaviors for your ads to reach. This can help you reach potential clients who may not have found you otherwise. As a real estate agent, one of your key tasks is to connect with potential clients and build relationships. One of the most feasible ways to do this in today's digital age is through social media.

You can also purchase mailing lists from various platforms like Melissa Data, targeting investors or residential owners. You can mail branded materials to them and if you can also obtain their email addresses, then you can hit them across several mediums for repeated visibility. Make your mailouts and social media ads visually appealing and informative. Use high-quality photos and videos of properties, and include clear calls-to-action that encourage viewers to click through to your website or contact you for more information. When you use retargeting ads to reach individuals who have already interacted with your content or website, you further increase the chances of conversion.

If you specialize in luxury properties, your target audience may be higher-income individuals with a taste for high-end living. Once you have identified your target audience, you can shape your social media content and advertisements to appeal specifically to them. Respond to comments and messages promptly. This shows that you value their interests and are committed to providing excellent customer service. You can also use social media to ask for recommendations and referrals from satisfied clients, which can help expand your reach even further. Testimonials are one of the best tools to enhance your brand and reputation.

Stay up-to-date with the constantly evolving world of social media. You'll want to keep track of new platforms and features and stay on top of best practices for engagement and content creation. Take classes, read books, and obtain training in marketing and advertising campaigns to increase your skills and help you retarget your specific audience.

For more tips on retargeting your audience, join our Facebook group by scanning this QR code.

CHAPTER 19 - INCREASING THE QUALITY, INCREASING THE COMPETITION

When you increase the quality of your marketing and services, you automatically increase the competition. When your competition is high, you can actually gain more business, more leads, reviews and referrals, and more opportunities. Take the time in your marketing efforts to be organized and professional in the small details so that you'll be organized and professional in the bigger vision, since it all leaves an impression on your client. Don't just use cell-phone pictures or throw together a marketing strategy haphazardly. Constantly strive for improvement to stand out in a competitive market. And by increasing the quality of your services and positioning yourself as an expert in the field, you will naturally attract more clients and grow your business.

You can increase the quality of your services by actively seeking feedback from your clients. This can help you identify areas for improvement and make necessary changes to better serve your clients in the future. Positive reviews and testimonials from satisfied clients can also attract new business and strengthen your reputation as a top-performing agent.

By positioning yourself as the go-to agent for a particular niche, you can differentiate yourself from competitors and attract clients who are seeking specialized services. You can create a tagline or motto that will help differentiate you from the rest of the agents in your field and use it in all your advertising efforts to maintain your unique brand.

Stay ahead of the game by staying up-to-date with market trends and real estate industry changes. This knowledge not only helps you advise your clients better but also allows you to adapt your strategies accordingly. Continuously learning and staying ahead of the curve enables you to remain competitive and consistently provide top-quality services.

Increasing the quality and competition as a real estate agent requires a combination of trust-building. Client feedback. Differentiation from competitors. Strong relationships with past clients. And of course, continuous learning. These tactics will elevate your business and position yourself as a top-performing agent in the industry. Don't be afraid to think outside the box and find unique ways to stand out in a crowded market: it could be the key to your success!

Continue to learn, adapt, and innovate - because that is what sets apart top-performing agents from the rest. And as always, stay true to your values and provide exceptional service to your clients - because in the end, it is their satisfaction that truly matters. The real estate market can be a challenging and ever-changing landscape, but with your dedication and hard work, you will rise above the competition and become the trusted expert and successful top-producer for your market.

Boost your success with superior marketing and higher quality services that will help you rise above the competition, attract increased business, leads, positive reviews, referrals, and other countless opportunities. You have the power to shape your own success as a real estate agent. So never stop learning, growing, and striving for excellence. That is the key to staying competitive and achieving long-term success in this industry. And with each new challenge and obstacle, you will only become stronger, wiser, and more resilient - making you a force to be reckoned with in the real estate market.

CHAPTER 20- SETTING EXPECTATIONS

Before taking on a new client, you'll want to set expectations for the buying or selling process. This includes outlining your role as their agent, the steps involved in the process, and any potential challenges that may arise. Be transparent and open about what to expect so that you can avoid misunderstandings and build stronger trust with your clients. This is one of the best ways to ensure a smooth home buying process before you start looking at homes, and especially before you are under contract with them.

During this talk, you can discuss aspects such as the client's motive, their budget, desired location and type of property, any specific features or amenities they may be looking for. You can also talk about potential challenges during the typical transaction deadline and what to expect at each step. Establish clear communication channels and set expectations for response times. This is the only way to avoid misunderstandings and ensure that both parties are on the same page throughout the transaction process.

In addition to being honest during the expectation talk, you'll need to follow through by communicating clearly and frequently with your clients throughout the transaction. This means responding promptly to their inquiries and providing regular updates on the progress of their transaction or listing. Doing so will not only demonstrate your professionalism but also alleviate any potential anxieties or doubts your clients may have through your consistent follow up.

Purchasing a home is one of the most significant financial decisions that someone can make in their lifetime. And as a first-time homebuyer, it's natural to feel overwhelmed and unsure about where to start or what to expect. Even for a seasoned investor, it can still be an emotional rollercoaster. Often, all they know is what their real estate agent tells them. While you are undoubtedly knowledgeable and experienced and will provide thorough answers to their questions as they arise, it's essential for your client to have a clear understanding of the process and information readily available before stepping into the middle of it. Having this conversation will also allow you to build a trusting relationship with your client, which is critical in such a significant transaction. It also helps set realistic expectations during such a complex and emotional process.

No matter how well you set expectations, objections will inevitably arise. These objections may stem from various factors, such as market conditions, financial constraints, or personal preferences. When they arise, you should handle these objections proactively and address them before they become major roadblocks by using the skills we've discussed in previous chapters. This not only helps you retain existing clients but also attracts new ones through positive word-of-mouth recommendations.

We talked earlier about actively listening to your clients when handling objections and addressing their concerns with empathy and in a calm and professional manner. Acknowledge their perspective and provide them with solutions or alternatives. Objections are not personal attacks, but rather opportunities for you to provide valuable information and insights. This not only shows that you understand their perspective but also helps build trust. Being knowledgeable about the local market and having data to support your recommendations can help alleviate any doubts or objections. You need to understand of their feelings, while also providing reassurance and guidance during any challenging situations.

When you discuss all aspects of the buying or selling process, including potential challenges or objections that may arise, it makes objections seem small when they do arise because you have already managed your clients' expectations appropriately.

Remember that setting expectations and addressing objections is not a one-time task, but rather an ongoing process that requires constant communication and understanding. Open communication, empathy, and proactive problem-solving are key to maintaining strong relationships with your clients as a real estate agent. Stay proactive, and you will build strong relationships with your clients and pave the way for long-term success in this industry.

Addressing objections is not a sign of weakness but rather an opportunity to showcase your expertise and provide exceptional service to your clients.

Be prepared and confident in handling objections to ensure a successful and satisfying experience for everyone involved in the real estate process. Let your communication skills shine through as you guide your clients towards their dream home.

To access examples of active listening and objection handling scripts, as well as an initial email template outlining expectations and next steps at the beginning of the transaction, join our Facebook group by scanning this QR code.

PART 5 - BOTTOM OF THE FUNNEL

The final stage of the funnel teaches you how to build rapport with your clientele, maintain their trust as you collaborate with business affiliates to bring your transactions from contracts to closings. This is the final stage of the funnel for the purified experience, and will teach you many skills on negotiation and leadership that will help guide your clients through the end of the funnel.

CHAPTER 21 - HOW TO NEGOTIATE WITHOUT BEING OFFENSIVE

Real estate agents have a tough job, constantly negotiating deals and sales for their clients. Negotiating can be tricky and difficult, especially when it comes to finding the right balance between assertiveness and aggressiveness. Oftentimes, agents may worry about coming off as being too pushy or offensive while trying to secure the best deal for their client. However, there are ways for real estate agents to negotiate without being offensive.

The first step towards down-to-earth negotiation is to listen attentively and understand what the other party wants. By actively listening, you can gather information about their needs and priorities, which will help you craft a deal that benefits both parties. This also shows respect towards the other party, making them more willing to work with you.

Building a good rapport with the other party can also go a long way in negotiation. You must establish trust and open communication to create an environment where both parties feel comfortable expressing their needs and concerns. This also helps in finding common ground and reaching a mutually beneficial agreement. Focus on the facts and present your arguments in a calm and logical manner so you can maintain a professional attitude throughout the negotiation process. Avoid personal attacks or emotional outbursts, as this can quickly turn a negotiation sour.

When you maintain a professional and respectful demeanor, you can avoid any offensive or derogatory language, as well as remain mindful of your body language and tone of voice. Remember that the goal is to reach a mutually beneficial agreement, not to win at all costs. It's all about collaboration, not competition.

Negotiating based on objective criteria, such as market trends and data, can also help take the emotion out of the process and lead to a more successful outcome. This also prevents any party from feeling like they are being taken advantage of, as decisions are based on concrete facts rather than personal opinions. Using language like "this is what we know," or "what I hear you saying is," can help clarify communication and lead the conversation.

Negotiation is all about the give and take. Stay open to compromising on certain aspects in order to reach a mutually beneficial agreement. This also shows that you are willing to work towards finding a solution that works for both parties, rather than just looking out for your own interests.

It's beneficial to know your client's bottom line and stick to it during negotiations. This refers to the minimum terms and conditions that they are willing to accept in a deal. Knowing this beforehand helps you stay focused and avoid making any hasty decisions that you (or they) may regret later on.

While it's important to know their bottom line, it's also helpful to keep an open mind during negotiations. Be willing to listen to the other party's perspectives and suggestions, as they may bring up valid points that your client may not have considered. This can also help in finding creative solutions that benefit both parties.

Fear and doubt play active roles in client objections. That's why it's vital to pinpoint the client's biggest fear so that you can speak truth to resolve their doubt and objections. The seller's biggest fear is often that they may not be able to find another home and be temporarily displaced or homeless without enough time to find the right house to move into next. The market could be so hot that they may not be able to find another home. With this in mind during the negotiations, a solution could be established to provide a longer space of time between the home selling and the seller's need to move. Maybe proposing a temporary occupancy agreement post-closing or another similar solution could ease the seller's pain. The buyer's fear and doubt can often range - but normally they arise during the inspection and due diligence period. Knowing what their fears are and addressing them with solutions during the negotiation process will provide them with a peace of mind.

Try to control the pace of negotiations by setting a timeline and sticking to it. This will help prevent any delays or unnecessary extensions, which could potentially lead to frustration from both parties. Controlling the pace of the conversation keeps the negotiation process focused and productive and under control.

Once an agreement has been reached, make sure to end the negotiations on a positive note. Thank the other party for their time and efforts and express your enthusiasm for working together in the future. This helps maintain a good relationship with the other party and sets a positive tone for any future interactions.

The goal is always to consider what the clients might need to make the deal a little sweeter. Maybe it's the right to request repairs, or to give more earnest money in multiple offer situations. When you receive an offer for one of your listings, you'll want to review the offer and make note of the purchase price, the closing date, any closing cost assistance requested, and any resale contingency, home inspection or other contingencies. Make any special note of stipulations and the time limit on the offer. You can input these numbers into a drafted Net Sheet that may help the seller understand how much they would walk away with after their closing cost assistance, home warranty, purchase price, commission, the loan pay-off, and other major costs associated with the transaction. Then present the offer to your client and if the client decides to accept, have the client sign the offer and then communicate to the buyer's agent. Keep in mind that any sellers beyond the average day-on-market statistic may be more willing to negotiate if they feel like their home is sitting on the market without much activity. Use these considerations in structuring your offers, counter offers, and proposals to plant seeds during the negotiation period. The real estate market is a skill-based market, so use these skills to craft what your client needs.

After the buyers have scheduled their inspections within the specified period in the contract, you will go over with them any repairs or replacements that may need to be completed prior to closing. Keep in mind that the sole job of the home inspector is to provide his client with a descriptive packet of everything small to great that he notices about the property, and if he didn't do this, he wouldn't be doing his job. This can often scare clients if they're not expecting it to be so vast - so make sure you help set their expectations beforehand.

Negotiating without being offensive is an advantageous skill for real estate agents to be successful and execute mutually beneficial deals. Navigate these negotiations with confidence and professionalism. Remember to stay calm, keep an open mind, and approach negotiations with respect and a focus on finding a win-win solution. Soon with practice and experience, this skill will become second nature and you'll be able to negotiate confidently in any situation.

For full access to a seller's net sheet and other tips on asking the right questions during the negotiations process, join our Facebook group community by scanning this QR code.

CHAPTER 22 - WHITE GLOVE SERVICE THROUGH TURBULENCE

White glove service goes above and beyond for clients, providing them with personalized attention and ensuring that every detail is taken care of. This level of service is especially favorable during times of turbulence in the real estate market.

Clients may feel more anxious and cautious about making decisions regarding their property during periods of uncertainty. This is where the white glove service approach can make a significant difference. Focus on finding solutions for clients rather than dwelling on the problem at hand to navigate through difficult situations with ease.

For instance, during a recession or an economic downturn, clients may feel hesitant to sell their properties due to the fear of not receiving a good price. By providing them with detailed market analysis and showcasing the potential benefits of selling at that time, agents can help alleviate these concerns and guide clients towards making a well-informed decision.

White glove service also involves taking care of all the details and paperwork associated with buying or selling a property. Agents who provide white glove service take the burden off their clients' shoulders and handle all necessary tasks with efficiency and professionalism. Remember: if you focus on the solution, you can solve the problem. But if you focus on the problem, you won't see the solution.

Creating unnecessary risk is a mistake that has been made countless times and has disastrous results. It can be difficult to remain calm when there are significant pressures and decisions to be made, but taking a more analytical approach and maintaining control over any aggression can make all the difference. Deliberate action will help to stabilize precarious situations. Whether personal or professional, controlling your emotions is a sensible and anticipatory measure that requires foresight and strength - and might just be the most valuable step in ensuring success rather than failure. Remember the facts over your feelings.

To be successful and provide the highest level of white glove service, your business needs an action plan and contingency plan that can handle the worst, the best, and the most likely situations. This will help you operate smoothly under high stakes and stressful situations. If your white glove action plan can't withstand the worst-case scenario, it's not a solid plan or high-quality service.

Embrace the reality: Nothing in business is perfect. No matter how confident you are in your game plan, always expect the unexpected. Prepare backup plans to handle any curveballs that come your way. Don't be caught off guard, be ready to adapt. Remember, even the best-laid plans can unravel without a safety net.

Just like in golf, businesses are equipped with a common set of tools. However, this does not guarantee equal success. Tiger Woods may use the same golf clubs as everyone else, but his outstanding performance sets him apart. Take ownership of your tools and strategies to cultivate expertise. By honing your skills, you can become the master of white glove service to clients as you pursue your business goals. Regardless of obstacles, every person has the same 24 hours in a day, yet success varies. It all boils down to how you utilize each precious hour, manage emotions, and handle problem solving scenarios.

Cultivate the ability to adapt calmly when things don't go as expected. This will help you discover alternative paths to achieve your goal and provide the same white glove service to clients, even in the face of adversity. Never abandon yourself, your team, or your business because of a challenge, and don't squander time when it matters the most. The quicker you can bring resolutions during times of crisis, the better for everyone. Stick to your strategy for the best, the worst, and the most probable outcomes so that you'll be ready to handle any unforeseen circumstances that may disrupt your initial plan or timeframe in the real estate transaction.

Focus on solutions rather than problems to go above and beyond for clients during turbulent times. This will help build strong relationships, set appropriate boundaries, carry out the necessary expectation talks with your clients, and establish yourself as a professional.

CHAPTER 23 - BUILDING RAPPORT & MAINTAINING TRUST

Building rapport and maintaining trust with your clients helps you secure more deals and establishes you as a reliable and trustworthy professional in the eyes of your clients. Building rapport with your clients means establishing a positive and trusting relationship with them. It involves creating an emotional connection that goes beyond just the transactional aspect of the business. Building personal connections with your clients can go a long way in maintaining trust. When you remember details about them and their special interests, and incorporate these into your interactions, they are more likely to appreciate you and bond with you. When they bond with you, they trust you and value your opinions, making it easier for you to guide them through the buying or selling process.

One of the key elements in building rapport is being genuine and authentic in your interactions with clients. People can sense when someone is not being sincere, so be yourself and let your personality shine through. Clear communication also plays a critical role in building rapport. To do this, you need to actively listen to your clients and ask questions to show that you are interested in understanding their needs and concerns.

Look for common interests or experiences that you share with your clients to create a common ground. This helps create a sense of familiarity and relatability, making it easier for them to connect with you on a personal level.

Buying or selling a property can be an emotional experience for clients. When you empathize with their feelings and show understanding, even if you may not agree with them, your responsiveness shows that you value your clients' time and concerns. It's constructive to promptly respond to calls, emails, and messages to maintain good communication and build trust. Be transparent about all aspects of the transaction, including any potential challenges or risks. And if you make a promise to your clients, make sure to follow through on it. This shows reliability and commitment, which are useful in building trust.

When you strive to provide value to your clients, you are always thinking about more ways to maintain their trust and earn their loyalty. So, pay attention to your clients' feedback and adapt accordingly. This shows that you value their opinions and are willing to make changes to better serve them. Take the time to understand their perspective and show genuine care for their needs and concerns by being punctual, respectful, and maintaining a positive attitude during your interactions.

The real estate industry is constantly evolving. Continuously educating yourself shows your commitment to providing the best service and techniques for your clients and can also help build trust in your expertise.

Like I mentioned previously, following up with your clients after a transaction is complete shows that you value their business and are committed to ensuring their satisfaction even after the deal is done. Maintaining communication with your clients even after a transaction is complete can help strengthen the relationship and lead to potential referrals or future business opportunities. Make yourself accessible to your clients, whether it's through email, phone, or in person meetings. This shows that you are readily available to address any concerns or questions they may have. Keep the lines of communication open to help build a long-lasting relationship.

Take the time to thank your clients for their business and referrals. This simple gesture can go a long way in showing your appreciation and strengthening the relationship. Take their feedback and suggestions into consideration and make any necessary changes to enhance the client experience. Consistency in communication, actions, and service is key in maintaining trust with clients. You will provide consistent and reliable service when you follow through on any promises or commitments made.

Don't be a pushy agent who rushes clients into something they're not ready to move into, and don't waste time looking at homes you know your client can't afford. Listen to their needs and work with them accordingly to build rapport and maintain their trust.

Chapter 24 - Treating the Co-op Agent as a Collaborator, Not a Competitor

Don't underestimate the value of a cooperative partnership in growing your business when you build strong relationships with clients and fellow agents in the real estate industry. One relationship to especially prioritize is that of the co-op agent, since this agent represents the buyer or seller in a transaction and collaborates with you to ensure a successful sale.

Co-op agents are collaborators in the real estate industry as they bring their own expertise and resources to a transaction. By working together, they can help ensure a smooth and successful sale for both parties involved. Unfortunately, there is often a misconception that co-op agents are competitors in the real estate market. This mindset can lead to tension and conflicts during transactions, which may ultimately harm both the buyer and seller.

To truly benefit from working with co-op agents, it is advantageous to shift this perspective and treat them as collaborators rather than competitors. Here are a few tips on how to do so:

- Communicate openly and rationally: Clear communication is key in any collaboration. Make sure to keep the co-op agent informed of any updates, changes, or concerns throughout the transaction.
- Share knowledge and resources: Co-op agents may have insights or connections that can benefit your client or help move the transaction forward. Be open to sharing your knowledge and resources with them as well.
- Work towards a win-win outcome: Instead of focusing on "winning" the deal, try to work towards a mutually beneficial outcome for both parties involved. This approach can lead to a stronger collaboration and better results for everyone.

You could even host classes together for first time home buyers or other clientele that would encourage the idea of collaboration over competition. The co-op agent can be a valuable friend, and business partner in future transactions, if you allow that relationship to foster.

Collaborating with other agents in the industry can also lead to the development of strong professional relationships. This can open up opportunities for future collaborations and referrals. When agents work together towards a common goal, the chances of successfully closing a transaction may increase. This can also result in a higher level of client satisfaction and positive reviews.

Let's keep the lines of communication open, share what we know, and help each other succeed in the real estate industry. Working together as collaborators, we can achieve greater success for both our clients and ourselves. By building a stronger community of real estate agents, one collaboration at a time, we can accomplish even more. Let's make it happen together.

CHAPTER 25 - TRANSACTION COORDINATION & CLOSINGS

The timeline of a real estate transaction can vary depending on the type of property, location, and other factors such as market conditions or loan types. Before your client should start looking for properties with you, you'll want to help get them pre-approved for a mortgage. This will give you an idea of how much they can afford and help you narrow down their search. Once they have been pre-approved and have a clear understanding of their budget, you can start looking for properties that meet their criteria. When you find a property that meets their needs and fits within their budget, they may want to make an offer. After the negotiations and terms of the sale have been established, the offer may be accepted and the transaction timelines begins.

Varying from state to state, the timeframes might be different but they will be generally outlined in the terms of the purchase and sale agreement. The buyer will typically turn in earnest money within the first week, complete their home inspections and due diligence within the first two weeks, and also officially apply for their loan and homeowners' insurance in that timeframe. The appraisal and title work are normally ordered during weeks two to three, and various other special stipulations or contingencies may occur during these weeks as well according to your state and contingencies.

About weeks four to five during the transaction, the appraisal should be received back with underwriting's approval on the loan, along with the title work and deed prepared. At this point the agents normally prepare their clients for closing day. When completed, the whole process takes between 21-45 days. If the transaction is cash instead of financing or waives certain contingencies, then often the transaction could close in 7-14 days as soon as the title work and deed are prepared. After all of the necessary documents and transferring ownership of the property has been completed, there are a few post-closing tasks that need to be completed as well. These may include setting up utilities, advising the client to change their address with the post office and updating their driver's license, apply for schools, and move in.

Stay connected with your clients by offering helpful maintenance tips for their new home. Keep them in the loop about upcoming community events and festivals in their area. And when the time is right, guide them through the process of refinancing or selling their property. Take it a step further by suggesting ways to maximize their investment, such as turning their garage into an apartment for extra rental income. Don't forget to mention the potential for Airbnb or other short-term rentals, if allowed by their neighborhood restrictions.

You want to make sure to add them to your mailing list and keep in touch with them after closing. You can also reach out to the client and see if they will be willing to record a testimonial video of your service to them that you could use for marketing purposes. When clients have a good experience, they are more willing to do these reviews for their agents.

Navigating the home buying process requires careful planning and collaboration with various professionals. From handling paperwork to managing timelines, you must be organized and communicative. With the right guidance, you can navigate through this successfully and help your client achieve their dream of homeownership.

The Transaction Coordinator's job is to take this process off of the agent's plate and collaborate with all parties. If a virtual assistant is hired or transaction coordination services are outsourced in this phase, they are an extension of your service to your client. You want to make sure they are high quality and reflect your level of 5-star service so that there is a seamless transition for your client between you and the transaction coordination.

PART 6 - CLIENT RETENTION AND REFERRALS

After business has left your funnel, it can become long lasting client retention and gain more referrals to start the filtration process again. However, if the final product isn't cared for correctly, it won't be retained. This last section of the book will review steps to retain past clients and utilize them to gain more business through the funnel.

Chapter 26 - Always Bringing Value

As a real estate agent, retaining clients and gaining referrals is key to your business's success. Not only does it ensure a steady stream of income, but it also helps you build a solid reputation in the industry.

Retaining clients should be a top priority for any real estate agent. It costs significantly less to retain an existing client than it does to acquire a new one. In fact, studies have shown that it can cost up to five times more to acquire a new customer than to retain a previous one.

Client retention leads to more referrals, further increasing your business. Satisfied clients are likely to recommend you to their loved ones, resulting in a positive cycle of more clients and referrals. This is a game-changer for your real estate career. One of the best ways to retain clients and gain more referrals is by providing exceptional customer service. This means going above and beyond for your clients, being responsive and attentive to their needs, and ensuring they have a positive experience throughout the entire buying or selling process. Make sure to communicate regularly with your clients, keep them updated on the progress of their transaction, and address any concerns or questions they may have in a timely manner. Remember, professionalism and courtesy leave a lasting impression.

Every client is unique and has different needs and preferences. To stand out from other real estate agents, personalize your approach with each client. Take the time to get to know them, their goals, and their priorities. This will help you modify your services to their specific needs and build a stronger relationship with them. I've highlighted the value of making an effort to stay in touch with your clients even after the sale or purchase has been finalized. This can be as simple as sending personalized holiday cards or checking in with them periodically to see how they're doing. By staying in touch, you show that you genuinely care about your clients and are invested in their well-being. This will not only lead to repeat business but also increase the likelihood of positive referrals and helps you with every stage of the funnel process.

Social media also allows you to connect with potential clients, showcase your listings, and share valuable information and advice in greater ways than ever before. However, it's not just about promoting yourself – utilize social media as a platform to engage with your clients. Share relevant content that they may find helpful, respond to their comments and messages, and create a community where they can interact with each other. This will help strengthen your relationships with current clients and attract potential clients through word-of-mouth recommendations.

Feedback leads to improvement and growth. Don't be afraid to ask your clients for feedback on their experience with you as their agent. This will not only show that you value their opinion, but it also gives you an opportunity to identify areas where you can improve. Constructive criticism can help you provide a better service in the future and potentially turn a dissatisfied client into a happy one. Positive feedback can serve as social proof for potential clients who may be considering working with you.

Receiving constructive criticism isn't bad! It may not be easy to receive, but it's necessary for breakthroughs and achieving your goals. Step out of your comfort zone, and don't shy away from the discomfort because it's a sign of progress. If you're serious about achieving success, be willing to ask the difficult questions, even if the answers aren't what you want to hear. Avoiding this step will only lead to a weak point in the future. If you truly desire victory, start asking the tough questions now to ensure success later on.

As we've discussed, buying or selling a home can be a stressful process, and your clients may need support even after the transaction is complete. Let them know that you are available for any questions or concerns they may have. You can also offer additional services such as providing recommendations for local contractors or home maintenance tips. This shows that you are committed to their satisfaction beyond just the sale, and it may lead to repeat business in the future.

Retaining clients and gaining referrals leads to success in the real estate industry. By utilizing social media, asking for feedback, and offering continued support, you can strengthen relationships with current clients and attract potential clients through positive word-of-mouth recommendations. Remember to always prioritize your clients' needs and provide exceptional customer service. This will not only lead to a successful career as a real estate agent but also create lasting relationships with satisfied clients.

CHAPTER 27 - SUPPORTING THE COMMUNITY

Being involved in the community not only helps real estate agents build their business but also allows them to give back to others. As a real estate agent, be an active member of the community you serve. Involvement in local organizations, charities, and events not only increases your visibility but also showcases your commitment to making a difference. This can also lead to potential clients seeing you as a trusted and reputable agent, which will lead to more business opportunities.

Many community organizations are always looking for volunteers to help with various projects, such as building homes, organizing fundraising events, or providing mentorship to youth in need. By utilizing your skills and knowledge in the real estate industry, you can make a meaningful impact and contribute towards improving the lives of others by volunteering your time and expertise.

Agents can also consider sponsoring or participating in local events and charities. This not only shows support for the community but also helps in building relationships with potential clients. By being present at these events, agents can network with other community members and showcase their passion for giving back.

Real estate agents can also use their platform to raise awareness about causes and issues within the community. By utilizing social media and other marketing strategies, agents can inform their audience about upcoming events, fundraisers, or volunteer opportunities. This not only helps in promoting the cause but also encourages others to get involved. Set the standard for leaving an impact on your local community.

Active involvement in the community allows agents to gain a deeper understanding of the local market and its needs. Agents can identify potential opportunities for growth and development within the community simply by being present and engaged and understanding the needs and preferences of local buyers and sellers.

As a real estate agent, giving back to the community not only benefits those in need but also boosts your reputation and builds strong relationships with potential clients. So don't wait, get involved and make a difference in your community by giving back to those who continually contribute to others.

Chapter 28 - Client Events & Giveaways

As a real estate agent, building relationships with clients expands your horizon for success. A great way to strengthen those relationships is by hosting client events and giveaways. Which provide not only an opportunity for you to connect with clients outside of the traditional real estate setting, but also showcase your brand and services.

Hosting client events allows you to interact with clients on a more personal level. It gives you the chance to get to know them better and understand their needs and preferences. This will lead to stronger client-agent relationships.

Hosting events can also help you differentiate yourself from other real estate agents in the market. You can leave a lasting impression on your clients and stand out from your competition by creating a unique and memorable event.

Discover the multitude of client events that real estate agents can organize, from trendy open house parties to informative seminars on real estate topics. Enhance your client relationships by hosting exclusive events styled to the season. Imagine a vibrant fall festival for your valued clients or capturing festive moments with Santa and lively gingerbread house competitions during the winter.

By offering prizes or incentives at your events, you can attract new clients and retain existing ones. This can help increase awareness of your brand and services and show clients that they are valued and appreciated. Giveaways can also attract potential clients who may be interested in your services. Exciting and unique giveaways can generate buzz and word-of-mouth marketing for your business.

To ensure the success of your client events and giveaways, here are some tips to keep in mind:

- Plan ahead: Make sure to plan well in advance to ensure a successful event or giveaway.

- Know your target audience: Customize your events and giveaways to appeal to your target audience.
- Use social media: Social media is a powerful tool for promoting and generating buzz for your events and giveaways.
- Partner with other businesses: Collaborating with other local businesses can help make your events and giveaways even more exciting and attract more clients.
- Follow up: After the event or giveaway, follow up with attendees and winners to maintain a positive relationship and potentially generate new business.

You can even create a Facebook group for your past clients to stay in touch with you and each other, and to easily invite them to others. In the world of real estate, it's all about building relationships and providing exceptional service. So don't be afraid to get creative and have some fun with your client events and giveaways!

For more ideas on client events and tips for event planning, join our Facebook group community by scanning this QR code.

CHAPTER 29- KEEPING IN TOUCH

As we've discussed, maintaining a good relationship with your clients even after the sale has closed not only helps with building trust and rapport but can also lead to potential referrals in the future. The more this sounds like a broken record, the more important you know it is!

You can keep in touch with them regularly through phone calls, emails, or even meeting up for coffee. Keeping in touch with your clients also shows that you genuinely care about them and their satisfaction with their purchase. Staying in touch allows you to stay top of mind for your clients and results in more positive reviews and recommendations for your services. They may not need your services now, but when they do in the future, they will remember the agent who kept in touch and provided exceptional service. Your clients may also know someone who is looking to buy or sell a property, and by keeping in touch, you are more likely to be the first agent that comes to mind when they make a referral. Staying in touch with your clients allows for continued networking opportunities, and increases your business tenfold.

Moreover, keeping in touch with your clients also provides an opportunity to update them on any changes or developments within the real estate market. This shows that you are knowledgeable and up-to-date, which can help build trust and credibility with your clients.

Maintaining communication with your clients even after the sale has closed builds lasting relationships, generating potential referrals, and staying top of mind for future real estate needs. Make sure to prioritize keeping in touch with your clients as part of your business strategy. Keep nurturing those client relationships for long-term success in the real estate industry. Your clients will appreciate the effort you put into maintaining communication, and it will ultimately benefit your business in the long run. The key to success in real estate is not just about closing deals, but also about fostering meaningful connections with your clients that last beyond a single transaction. With consistent communication and exceptional service, you can create a loyal client base that will bring you continued success in the real estate industry. Be proactive and intentional about staying connected with your clients – it will pay off in the long run. Make it a habit to keep in touch regularly and you'll see the benefits in your business.

CHAPTER 30- REVIEWS AND REFERRALS

Whether you are a new real estate agent or have been in the business for years, one thing remains constant – your reputation is connected to your success. People trust reviews and referrals from friends and family more than any other form of advertising. It's no secret that word-of-mouth marketing is one of the most convenient ways to grow your business.

A positive review or referral from a satisfied client can go a long way in building your credibility and attracting new clients. In today's digital age, where online reviews and social media play a significant role in shaping consumer decisions, having positive reviews and referrals highlights your reputation and proves your skills to future clients.

So, how can you get more reviews and referrals? Here are some tips to help you ask for them. The best time to ask for a review is when your client is happy and satisfied with your services. Normally after a successful sale or closing, or even during the process of buying or selling a property. Asking for a review at this time will increase the chances of getting a positive response.

When asking for reviews, make sure to personalize your request. Use your client's name and mention specific details about their experience working with you. This shows that you value their opinion and are not just sending out a generic request. It also subtly gives the client the ideas and language to use in their review. You can prompt the response you're looking for by asking the right questions. For example, "Would you mind sharing we walked you through the turbulence of the inspection and negotiation period with white glove service?" More than likely, their response will be "My agent walked me through the turbulence of the inspection and negotiation period with white glove service." Especially if your request was for their testimonial in a video format.

Make the process of leaving a review as simple and straightforward as possible. Provide your clients with clear instructions on where and how to leave a review, whether it's on your website, social media platforms, or third-party review sites. Don't be afraid to follow up with your clients if you don't hear back from them after your initial request. A gentle reminder can go a long way in getting that much-needed review.

Make it known to your clients that you appreciate referrals and that they are a focal part of your business. This will encourage them to refer their friends, family, and colleagues to you. Consider offering incentives for referrals, such as a discount on their next transaction or a gift card. This not only shows your appreciation but also gives clients an added incentive to refer you.

Asking for reviews and referrals should be an integral part of any real estate agent's business strategy. Not only do they help build your reputation and credibility, but they also bring in new clients and potential leads. Don't be afraid to ask for reviews and referrals, and always show your appreciation to those who take the time to leave a review or refer you to others. Remember, word-of-mouth is one of the most powerful marketing tools in the real estate world.

CONCLUSION

In my book, *Forged in Fire: 50 Fighting Tactics to Help Your Business Succeed*, I emphasize the power of hard work over talent, and consistency over motivation. Take maintaining a healthy diet and exercise routine, for example. It's much more rational to stick to a consistent regiment for a whole year, regardless of how you feel, rather than relying on fleeting motivation from a New Year's resolution. By implementing consistency into any habit or schedule, you're guaranteed to find success. You may not realize it, but you're already a creature of habit. You perform certain actions in a specific order, almost automatically. When you remain consistent in doing things you may not initially enjoy, they become second nature. In no time, you won't even be aware that you're doing what you once dreaded because it will become such an integral part of your everyday routine. Consistency reigns supreme over motivation. Embrace consistency, even with tasks you may initially despise, and they'll transform into ingrained habits.

Create a foolproof plan to break your bad habits by consistently sticking to a scheduled routine instead of solely relying on your fleeting motivation. For example, if you want to stop biting your nails, actively engage your fingers in a different activity, like tapping the table or sitting on your hands, every time you feel the urge to bite. By consistently replacing the old habit with a new action, you'll break the habit without relying on momentary motivation or fleeting desires to quit.

Don't rely on your emotions to make or break habits - they're not consistent. Instead, practice discipline and strengthen your willpower to do the things you don't want to do, and stick to your schedule even when you don't feel like it. Consistency is more powerful than motivation, and it trumps our emotions. While relying on our ever-changing moods can be a recipe for disaster, we can harness consistency and discipline to break free from the chains of inconsistency and embrace a steadfast schedule. Consistency is the key to success.

Consistency is the key ingredient to achieving prospecting, sales, and overall success in the real estate business. By staying committed and disciplined, you'll gain valuable knowledge and experience that sets you apart. As you consistently practice this, it becomes second nature and leads to automatic habits that pave the way for success.

Renowned business coach, Coach David Keesee, aptly refers to inconsistent individuals as "try babies" - those who give up easily when not seeing immediate results or lose steam when instant gratification fails to materialize. Don't fall into this trap; remember that true success is a result of ongoing dedication. Remember, any approach can be effective as long as you stay the course. Success awaits those who embrace the power of consistency, so embrace consistency and watch as anything becomes possible.

You could be consistent with a bad idea that should not naturally bring success, but with consistency you will find a way to make it work. Don't be discouraged by initial setbacks – with determination and perseverance, you can make any idea work. Give any system or idea at least six months to prove itself before considering alternatives. But don't waste time on half-hearted attempts.

Athletes who are consistent in their training schedules (whether or not they feel like it) will be consistent in their success. Consistency is a systematic approach to winning, and is the most valuable aspect in any business. Don't leave your success to chance, grab hold of the transformative power of the tactics outlined in this book and forge your strategic path to victory. Embrace the game-changing secret that separates the winners from the crowd - consistency.

Ensure that your business is consistent with all systems and procedures in this funnel diagram for six months at least. Then after six months you have enough information to step back and properly assess if any aspect of the systems and procedures needs to be tweaked for you or your team in order to optimize efficiency.

If your business is consistent, then it will beat out other businesses who fail to be consistent. Consistency is a tool that surprisingly seems to elude most real estate agents and teams. While agents are constantly experimenting with new marketing tactics and strategies, they often overlook the power of staying consistent. Instead, they rely on short bursts of motivation to propel them forward. But let's face it, this approach isn't sustainable and threatens the survival of any business, especially in a market that's constantly in flux.

Refuse to rely on motivating morale to drive your team forward, and be consistent in your systems, procedures, and habits to achieve your goals and success. Don't let fleeting motivation dictate your achievements – become a master of consistency and unleash your full potential.

Transforming yourself and your business requires a radical shift. Push your limits beyond what I've outlined in this book. Enhance your strategies with *Forged in Fire: 50 Fighting Tactics to Help Your Business Succeed.* Demand absolute accountability within your company, leaving no room for mediocrity. Challenge and inspire each other. Embrace continuous learning. Cultivate a positive mindset. Never give up. Develop the discipline to tackle uncomfortable tasks by starting your day early and harnessing your willpower. Get ready to unleash your true potential and create a thriving future.

This all may be uncomfortable, but the end product will be 100 times better than anything you can imagine, both in business and in life. By applying these straightforward strategies, leaders, entrepreneurs, and ambitious individuals can redefine their path to success.

Expectations will shift. Outcomes will transform. Mindsets will evolve. Take your customer service to new heights. Cultivate a positive, knowledgeable, and disciplined mindset. Realign focus on the ultimate mission, vision, values, and strengths. Embark on the road to success. It's within your reach! The simplicity is astounding, and if others can do it, so can you. There are no barriers holding you back except your own self. Achieving business success is within your grasp, so the only way to prove me wrong is by not taking action or by not giving it your all. Take the leap and witness the extraordinary.

Don't let someone else steal your victory. Take control of your own growth and success and implement the discipline and accountability necessary to reach new heights in both your personal and professional life. Don't let someone else outshine you because you weren't willing to fight for your dreams. Release yourself from the grip of self-limiting beliefs and stop listening to the lies you tell yourself that hold you back from seizing great opportunities and attaining greater success.

Break free from negative influences that hinder your mindset and surround yourself with positivity. Watch as your mindset shifts towards greater achievements. Reject the idea that you've reached your peak of success – it's a self-fulfilling prophecy that will keep you trapped. Embrace the fact that you can always push harder, work smarter, and surpass your own expectations.

Tap into your untapped potential. Believe that you are capable of more than you think. With determination and dedicated effort, you can achieve greatness. Take a moment to reflect on this powerful truth: when you increase consistency and discipline in one area of your life, you naturally elevate it across all aspects. Step by step, you hold the power to break free from self-imposed limitations and seize incredible opportunities waiting for you.

Unleash your potential with the power of the funnel diagram. Transform into a positive and humble leader, achieving what you once thought impossible. The journey starts now, by shifting your mindset to shape your outcomes. The amount of effort you put in will directly impact your results. Invest only half-hearted effort, and your returns will be minimal. But with full dedication, you'll experience a transformative 100% return on your time, energy, and discipline. Don't just take my word for it, try it for yourself. Embrace the fight for success. Push yourself with unyielding determination, sweat and tears until you become the hardest worker in any room. Climb new ladders to reach greater heights of achievement. Remember, only you have the power to change your mindset – no one else can do it for you. Take ownership of it. Embrace the fight and emerge victorious.